50 Cooking with Kids Recipes for Home

By: Kelly Johnson

Table of Contents

- Pancakes
- Fruit kebabs
- Mini pizzas
- Smoothies
- Macaroni and cheese
- Chicken nuggets
- Vegetable stir-fry
- Tacos
- Homemade granola bars
- Quesadillas
- Pasta salad
- Stuffed peppers
- Rice crispy treats
- Banana bread
- Fruit salad
- Muffins (blueberry, banana, etc.)
- Veggie wraps
- Cheese and vegetable frittata
- Bread rolls
- Baked potato wedges
- Sushi rolls
- Grilled cheese sandwiches
- Chicken skewers
- Oatmeal cookies
- Mini meatloaves
- Veggie burgers
- Berry crumble
- Tortilla chips and guacamole
- Ratatouille
- Breaded fish fillets
- Rice pudding
- Stuffed mushrooms
- Garlic bread
- Chicken pot pie
- Cornbread
- Mini quiches

- Beef stew
- Pumpkin soup
- Scones
- Pita pockets with hummus
- Chocolate-dipped fruit
- Apple crisps
- Baked apples
- Spinach and cheese triangles
- Lentil soup
- Stuffed zucchini boats
- Energy balls
- Potato pancakes
- Rainbow salad
- Fruit crêpes

Pancakes

Ingredients:

- 1 cup all-purpose flour
- 2 tablespoons sugar
- 1 teaspoon baking powder
- 1/2 teaspoon baking soda
- 1/4 teaspoon salt
- 3/4 cup milk
- 1/4 cup plain yogurt (or use 1 cup milk instead of milk + yogurt)
- 1 large egg
- 2 tablespoons melted butter (plus extra for cooking)
- 1 teaspoon vanilla extract (optional)

Instructions:

1. **Prepare the batter:**
    - In a large mixing bowl, whisk together the flour, sugar, baking powder, baking soda, and salt.
2. **Combine wet ingredients:**
    - In another bowl or large measuring cup, whisk together the milk, yogurt (if using), egg, melted butter, and vanilla extract (if using).
3. **Mix it all together:**
    - Pour the wet ingredients into the dry ingredients and gently mix until just combined. It's okay if there are a few lumps; overmixing can make the pancakes tough.
4. **Cook the pancakes:**
    - Heat a griddle or non-stick skillet over medium heat and lightly grease with butter.
    - Pour about 1/4 cup of batter for each pancake onto the griddle. Use the back of a spoon or ladle to spread the batter into a round shape.
5. **Flip and cook:**
    - Cook until bubbles form on the surface of the pancake and the edges look set, about 2-3 minutes.
    - Flip the pancake and cook until golden brown on the other side, about 1-2 minutes more.
6. **Serve:**
    - Transfer the pancakes to a plate and keep warm. Repeat with the remaining batter, greasing the griddle as needed.
7. **Enjoy:**
    - Serve the pancakes warm with toppings like maple syrup, fresh fruits, whipped cream, or chocolate chips if desired.

Cooking pancakes together is not only delicious but also a great opportunity to teach kids about measuring ingredients, mixing batter, and cooking on a stovetop with supervision. Enjoy your pancakes!

Fruit kebabs

Ingredients:

- Assorted fruits (such as strawberries, pineapple, grapes, kiwi, melon, and banana)
- Wooden skewers or bamboo sticks

Instructions:

1. **Prepare the fruits:**
   - Wash all the fruits thoroughly.
   - Cut larger fruits like pineapple, melon, and kiwi into bite-sized cubes or slices.
   - Remove stems from strawberries and cut larger grapes in half if desired.
2. **Assemble the kebabs:**
   - Take a wooden skewer or bamboo stick and thread on pieces of fruit in any order you like. Alternate colors and types of fruit to make the kebabs colorful and appealing.
3. **Serve:**
   - Arrange the fruit kebabs on a platter or plate.
   - Optionally, you can drizzle with honey or a squeeze of lemon juice for extra flavor, though this step is optional depending on your preference.
4. **Enjoy:**
   - Fruit kebabs can be enjoyed immediately as a snack or dessert. They're perfect for parties, playdates, or any time kids want a healthy and delicious treat!

Tips:

- Be cautious with sharp skewers, especially with younger children. Consider using blunt-tipped skewers or let kids assemble without the skewers.
- You can also involve kids in choosing and preparing the fruits, which adds to the fun and encourages healthy eating habits.

Fruit kebabs are versatile, colorful, and a great way to get kids excited about eating fruits.

Mini pizzas

Ingredients:

- English muffins or small pizza crusts (store-bought or homemade)
- Pizza sauce (store-bought or homemade)
- Shredded mozzarella cheese
- Assorted toppings such as:
    - Sliced pepperoni
    - Diced bell peppers
    - Sliced mushrooms
    - Diced onions
    - Sliced olives
    - Cooked sausage or ground beef
    - Pineapple chunks
    - Fresh basil leaves (optional)
    - Any other toppings your child enjoys!

Instructions:

1. **Preheat the oven:**
    - Preheat your oven to 400°F (200°C).
2. **Prepare the toppings:**
    - Prepare all the toppings by chopping or slicing them into small pieces. Set them aside in separate bowls.
3. **Assemble the mini pizzas:**
    - If using English muffins, split them in half. If using small pizza crusts, place them on a baking sheet.
    - Spread a spoonful of pizza sauce onto each muffin half or crust, leaving a small border around the edges.
4. **Add toppings:**
    - Let your child sprinkle shredded mozzarella cheese over the sauce.
    - Now comes the fun part! Let your child choose their favorite toppings and arrange them on top of the cheese.
5. **Bake the mini pizzas:**
    - Place the assembled mini pizzas on a baking sheet and transfer to the preheated oven.
    - Bake for about 10-12 minutes, or until the cheese is melted and bubbly, and the crust is golden brown.
6. **Cool and serve:**
    - Allow the mini pizzas to cool for a few minutes before serving.
    - Serve them warm and enjoy!

Tips:

- Supervise younger children when using the oven or handling hot ingredients.
- Encourage creativity by letting kids experiment with different combinations of toppings.
- Mini pizzas are great for parties, after-school snacks, or as a meal accompanied by a salad or veggies.

Making mini pizzas is not only a delicious activity but also a great way to teach kids about cooking basics like spreading, sprinkling, and assembling. Enjoy making and eating these personalized mini pizzas together!

Smoothies

Ingredients:

- 1 cup frozen mixed berries (strawberries, blueberries, raspberries)
- 1 ripe banana, peeled and sliced
- 1 cup plain yogurt (Greek yogurt or regular yogurt)
- 1/2 cup milk (adjust quantity based on desired consistency)
- 1-2 tablespoons honey or maple syrup (optional, for sweetness)
- 1/2 teaspoon vanilla extract (optional)

Instructions:

1. **Prepare the ingredients:**
   - If using fresh berries, wash them thoroughly. Otherwise, if using frozen berries, no preparation is needed other than measuring them out.
   - Peel and slice the banana.
2. **Blend the smoothie:**
   - In a blender, combine the frozen mixed berries, sliced banana, plain yogurt, milk, honey or maple syrup (if using), and vanilla extract (if using).
3. **Blend until smooth:**
   - Secure the lid on the blender and blend the ingredients until smooth and creamy. If the mixture is too thick, you can add a little more milk to adjust the consistency.
4. **Serve:**
   - Pour the smoothie into glasses.
   - Optionally, you can garnish with fresh berries or a slice of banana on the rim of the glass.
5. **Enjoy:**
   - Serve the smoothies immediately while cold and refreshing!

Tips:

- You can customize this basic smoothie recipe by adding other fruits like mango, pineapple, or spinach (for a green smoothie).
- Encourage kids to help measure and pour ingredients into the blender, under supervision.
- Smoothies are a great way to sneak in fruits and dairy into kids' diets in a fun and delicious way.

Smoothies are versatile, and you can adjust the ingredients based on what fruits and flavors your child enjoys. Have fun experimenting with different combinations and creating healthy and tasty smoothies together!

Macaroni and cheese

Ingredients:

- 2 cups elbow macaroni (or any pasta shape you prefer)
- 2 tablespoons butter
- 2 tablespoons all-purpose flour
- 1 1/2 cups milk
- 2 cups shredded cheddar cheese (or a mix of cheddar and mozzarella)
- 1/2 teaspoon salt
- 1/4 teaspoon black pepper
- 1/4 teaspoon garlic powder (optional)
- 1/4 teaspoon paprika (optional)
- 1/4 cup breadcrumbs (optional, for topping)

Instructions:

1. **Cook the pasta:**
   - Cook the elbow macaroni according to the package instructions in a large pot of salted boiling water until al dente. Drain and set aside.
2. **Make the cheese sauce:**
   - In the same pot (or a separate saucepan), melt the butter over medium heat.
   - Stir in the flour and cook for 1-2 minutes, stirring constantly, to make a roux.
3. **Add the milk:**
   - Gradually whisk in the milk, stirring constantly to avoid lumps. Cook until the mixture thickens slightly, about 5 minutes.
4. **Add the cheese:**
   - Reduce the heat to low. Stir in the shredded cheese, a little at a time, until melted and smooth.
5. **Season the sauce:**
   - Stir in the salt, black pepper, garlic powder (if using), and paprika (if using). Taste and adjust seasonings as needed.
6. **Combine pasta and sauce:**
   - Add the cooked pasta to the cheese sauce and stir until well coated and heated through.
7. **Serve:**
   - Optionally, you can sprinkle breadcrumbs over the top for a crispy topping.
   - Serve the macaroni and cheese hot, straight from the pot.

Tips:

- For extra creaminess, you can add a splash of heavy cream or more milk to the cheese sauce.
- Feel free to customize the cheese blend with your favorite cheeses, such as gouda, fontina, or Monterey Jack.

- You can also add cooked bacon, diced ham, or steamed broccoli to the macaroni and cheese for additional flavors and textures.

Homemade macaroni and cheese is a comforting dish that's perfect for a family dinner or a fun cooking activity with kids. Enjoy this creamy and cheesy goodness together!

Chicken nuggets

Ingredients:

- 1 lb boneless, skinless chicken breasts or thighs, cut into bite-sized pieces
- 1 cup all-purpose flour
- 2 eggs, beaten
- 1 cup breadcrumbs (plain or seasoned)
- 1/2 cup grated Parmesan cheese (optional, for extra flavor)
- 1 teaspoon salt
- 1/2 teaspoon black pepper
- 1/2 teaspoon garlic powder
- Cooking oil (vegetable oil or canola oil) for frying

Instructions:

1. **Prepare the chicken:**
    - Cut the chicken breasts or thighs into bite-sized pieces, about 1 to 1.5 inches in size.
2. **Set up the coating station:**
    - In one shallow bowl or plate, place the flour seasoned with salt, pepper, and garlic powder.
    - In another bowl, beat the eggs.
    - In a third bowl or plate, mix together the breadcrumbs and grated Parmesan cheese (if using).
3. **Coat the chicken pieces:**
    - Dredge each piece of chicken in the flour mixture, shaking off any excess.
    - Dip the floured chicken into the beaten eggs, allowing any excess egg to drip off.
    - Coat the chicken in the breadcrumb mixture, pressing gently to adhere the breadcrumbs to the chicken.
4. **Heat the oil:**
    - In a large skillet or frying pan, heat about 1/2 inch of cooking oil over medium-high heat until hot but not smoking. You can also use a deep fryer if you have one.
5. **Fry the chicken nuggets:**
    - Carefully place the coated chicken pieces into the hot oil in batches, making sure not to overcrowd the pan.
    - Fry the nuggets for about 3-4 minutes per side, or until golden brown and cooked through. The internal temperature should reach 165°F (74°C).
6. **Drain and serve:**
    - Remove the cooked chicken nuggets from the oil using a slotted spoon or tongs and place them on a plate lined with paper towels to drain excess oil.
7. **Serve and enjoy:**
    - Serve the homemade chicken nuggets warm with your favorite dipping sauces such as ketchup, honey mustard, barbecue sauce, or ranch dressing.

Tips:

- To make healthier chicken nuggets, you can bake them in the oven instead of frying. Preheat the oven to 400°F (200°C) and bake on a greased baking sheet for about 15-20 minutes, turning halfway through, until golden and cooked through.
- Get kids involved in the coating process! It's fun for them to dip the chicken pieces in the different coatings.
- You can freeze any leftover cooked chicken nuggets for later. Reheat them in the oven for crispy nuggets.

Homemade chicken nuggets are a crowd-pleaser and a great way to control the ingredients. Enjoy making and eating these crispy nuggets with your family!

Vegetable stir-fry

Ingredients:

- 2 cups mixed vegetables (such as bell peppers, broccoli florets, carrots, snap peas, mushrooms, and baby corn)
- 1 tablespoon vegetable oil or sesame oil
- 2 cloves garlic, minced
- 1-inch piece of ginger, peeled and minced (optional)
- Salt and pepper, to taste
- Soy sauce or tamari, for seasoning (optional)
- Cooked rice or noodles, for serving

Instructions:

1. **Prepare the vegetables:**
   - Wash and cut the vegetables into bite-sized pieces. You can use any combination of vegetables you like or have on hand.
2. **Heat the oil:**
   - Heat the vegetable oil or sesame oil in a large skillet or wok over medium-high heat.
3. **Sauté the aromatics:**
   - Add the minced garlic and ginger (if using) to the hot oil. Stir-fry for about 30 seconds until fragrant, being careful not to burn them.
4. **Stir-fry the vegetables:**
   - Add the mixed vegetables to the skillet. Stir-fry for 3-5 minutes, or until the vegetables are tender-crisp. You want them to be cooked but still vibrant and slightly crunchy.
5. **Season the stir-fry:**
   - Season the vegetables with salt, pepper, and soy sauce or tamari (if using), to taste. Adjust the seasoning according to your preference.
6. **Serve:**
   - Serve the vegetable stir-fry immediately over cooked rice or noodles.

Tips:

- You can add protein such as tofu, chicken, shrimp, or beef to the stir-fry. Cook the protein first before adding the vegetables.
- Encourage kids to help with washing and cutting the vegetables (under supervision) and stirring them in the skillet.
- Customize the stir-fry with your family's favorite vegetables and flavors. You can also add sesame seeds or chopped green onions for garnish.

Vegetable stir-fry is a nutritious and versatile dish that's great for a quick weeknight dinner or a fun cooking activity with kids. Enjoy the vibrant colors and flavors of this delicious stir-fry!

Tacos

Ingredients:

For the taco filling:

- 1 lb ground beef or ground turkey
- 1 tablespoon vegetable oil
- 1 small onion, finely chopped
- 2 cloves garlic, minced
- 1 tablespoon chili powder
- 1 teaspoon ground cumin
- 1/2 teaspoon paprika
- 1/2 teaspoon dried oregano
- Salt and pepper, to taste
- 1/2 cup tomato sauce or diced tomatoes

For serving:

- Hard or soft taco shells
- Shredded lettuce
- Diced tomatoes
- Shredded cheese (cheddar or Mexican blend)
- Sliced jalapeños (optional)
- Sour cream
- Salsa or pico de gallo
- Guacamole or diced avocado
- Lime wedges

Instructions:

1. **Prepare the taco filling:**
    - Heat the vegetable oil in a large skillet over medium-high heat.
    - Add the chopped onion and cook until softened, about 3-4 minutes.
    - Add the minced garlic and cook for 1 minute until fragrant.
2. **Cook the ground meat:**
    - Add the ground beef or turkey to the skillet. Cook, breaking up the meat with a spoon, until browned and cooked through.
3. **Season the filling:**
    - Stir in the chili powder, ground cumin, paprika, dried oregano, salt, and pepper. Cook for another minute to toast the spices.
4. **Add tomato sauce:**
    - Pour in the tomato sauce or diced tomatoes with their juices. Stir to combine and simmer for 5-10 minutes, until the sauce thickens slightly and flavors meld. Taste and adjust seasoning if needed.

5. **Assemble the tacos:**
    - Heat the taco shells according to package instructions, if using hard shells.
    - Fill each taco shell with a spoonful of the meat mixture.
6. **Add toppings:**
    - Let kids customize their tacos with shredded lettuce, diced tomatoes, shredded cheese, sliced jalapeños (if using), sour cream, salsa or pico de gallo, guacamole or diced avocado, and a squeeze of lime juice.
7. **Serve and enjoy:**
    - Serve the tacos immediately while warm and let everyone enjoy their delicious creations!

Tips:

- You can substitute the ground beef or turkey with shredded chicken or beans for a vegetarian option.
- Set up a taco bar with all the toppings in separate bowls so everyone can build their tacos just the way they like them.
- Encourage kids to help with assembling their tacos, which makes it a fun and interactive mealtime activity.

Tacos are not only tasty but also a great way to introduce kids to different flavors and textures. Enjoy making and eating these delicious tacos together!

Homemade granola bars

Ingredients:

- 2 cups old-fashioned oats
- 1 cup crispy rice cereal (or another type of cereal)
- 1/2 cup chopped nuts (such as almonds, pecans, or walnuts)
- 1/2 cup dried fruit (such as cranberries, raisins, or chopped apricots)
- 1/4 cup honey
- 1/4 cup maple syrup (or additional honey)
- 1/4 cup creamy peanut butter (or almond butter)
- 1 teaspoon vanilla extract
- 1/4 teaspoon salt
- 1/2 cup chocolate chips (optional, for drizzling or mixing in)

Instructions:

1. **Prepare the dry ingredients:**
   - In a large bowl, combine the oats, crispy rice cereal, chopped nuts, and dried fruit. Mix well to combine.
2. **Make the binder mixture:**
   - In a small saucepan over medium heat, combine the honey, maple syrup (or additional honey), peanut butter, vanilla extract, and salt. Stirring constantly, heat the mixture until it's smooth and well combined.
3. **Combine wet and dry ingredients:**
   - Pour the warm honey mixture over the dry ingredients in the bowl. Mix thoroughly until all the dry ingredients are coated evenly with the sticky mixture.
4. **Add optional chocolate chips:**
   - If using chocolate chips, you can stir them into the warm granola mixture at this point, or reserve them for drizzling on top later.
5. **Press into a pan:**
   - Line an 8x8 inch baking dish with parchment paper or foil, leaving some overhang for easy removal.
   - Transfer the granola mixture into the prepared dish. Use a spatula or your hands to press the mixture firmly and evenly into the pan.
6. **Chill and set:**
   - Place the pan in the refrigerator for at least 2 hours, or until the granola bars are firm and set.
7. **Cut into bars:**
   - Once chilled, lift the granola slab out of the pan using the overhanging parchment paper or foil.
   - Use a sharp knife to cut the slab into bars of your desired size and shape.
8. **Optional: Drizzle with chocolate (if desired):**
   - Melt chocolate chips in a microwave-safe bowl in 30-second intervals, stirring in between until smooth.

- Drizzle the melted chocolate over the cooled granola bars. Let the chocolate set before serving.
9. **Store and enjoy:**
    - Store the homemade granola bars in an airtight container at room temperature for up to a week, or in the refrigerator for longer freshness.

Tips:

- You can customize these granola bars by adding different nuts, seeds, or dried fruits according to your preference.
- For nut-free options, you can omit the nuts or substitute with seeds like sunflower seeds or pumpkin seeds.
- Letting kids help with mixing, pressing into the pan, and drizzling chocolate can make this a fun and educational kitchen activity.

Homemade granola bars are a wholesome snack that's perfect for school lunches, afternoon snacks, or any time you need a quick and nutritious bite. Enjoy making these with your kids and savoring the delicious results!

Quesadillas

Ingredients:

- 4 large flour tortillas
- 2 cups shredded cheese (cheddar, Monterey Jack, or a blend)
- Optional fillings:
    - Cooked chicken, shredded
    - Cooked vegetables (such as bell peppers, onions, or mushrooms)
    - Beans (black beans or refried beans)
    - Salsa or diced tomatoes
    - Sour cream
    - Guacamole or sliced avocado
    - Sliced jalapeños (for those who like spice)

Instructions:

1. **Prepare the fillings (if using):**
    - If you're adding any fillings like cooked chicken, vegetables, or beans, make sure they are cooked and ready to use.
2. **Assemble the quesadillas:**
    - Lay out two tortillas on a clean surface.
    - Sprinkle shredded cheese evenly over one side of each tortilla.
    - If adding any fillings, distribute them evenly over the cheese on one of the tortillas.
3. **Top with second tortilla:**
    - Place the other tortilla (cheese-side down) on top of the filled tortilla to create a sandwich.
4. **Cook the quesadillas:**
    - Heat a large skillet or griddle over medium heat. Place one quesadilla into the skillet and cook for about 2-3 minutes, or until the bottom is golden brown and crispy.
5. **Flip and cook the other side:**
    - Carefully flip the quesadilla using a spatula. Cook the other side for another 2-3 minutes, or until golden brown and the cheese is melted.
6. **Repeat with remaining quesadillas:**
    - Remove the cooked quesadilla from the skillet and place it on a cutting board. Let it cool for a minute before cutting into wedges.
    - Repeat the cooking process with the remaining quesadillas.
7. **Serve:**
    - Serve the quesadilla wedges warm, accompanied by optional toppings such as salsa, sour cream, guacamole, or sliced avocado.

Tips:

- Customize the quesadillas with your favorite fillings and cheese combinations.
- You can make mini quesadillas using smaller tortillas for kids' lunches or parties.
- For a healthier option, use whole wheat tortillas and add more vegetables and lean protein.

Quesadillas are versatile and make for a satisfying meal that kids can enjoy making and eating. They're great for busy weeknights or whenever you're craving a quick and delicious dish!

Pasta salad

Ingredients:

- 8 oz (about 2 cups) pasta of your choice (penne, rotini, fusilli, etc.)
- 1 cup cherry tomatoes, halved
- 1/2 cucumber, diced
- 1/2 bell pepper (any color), diced
- 1/4 cup red onion, finely chopped
- 1/4 cup black olives, sliced (optional)
- 1/4 cup crumbled feta cheese (optional)
- 1/4 cup chopped fresh parsley or basil (optional)

For the dressing:

- 1/3 cup extra-virgin olive oil
- 2 tablespoons red wine vinegar or balsamic vinegar
- 1 clove garlic, minced (optional)
- 1 teaspoon Dijon mustard (optional)
- Salt and pepper, to taste

Instructions:

1. **Cook the pasta:**
   - Cook the pasta according to package instructions in a large pot of salted boiling water until al dente. Drain and rinse under cold water to stop the cooking process. Drain well.
2. **Prepare the vegetables:**
   - While the pasta is cooking, prepare the vegetables by chopping the cherry tomatoes, cucumber, bell pepper, red onion, and any other vegetables you're using.
3. **Make the dressing:**
   - In a small bowl, whisk together the olive oil, red wine vinegar or balsamic vinegar, minced garlic (if using), Dijon mustard (if using), salt, and pepper until well combined.
4. **Combine everything:**
   - In a large bowl, combine the cooked and cooled pasta with the chopped vegetables, black olives (if using), crumbled feta cheese (if using), and chopped parsley or basil (if using).
5. **Add the dressing:**
   - Pour the dressing over the pasta and vegetables. Toss gently to coat everything evenly with the dressing.
6. **Chill and serve:**
   - Cover the pasta salad and refrigerate for at least 1 hour to allow the flavors to meld together.

7. **Serve:**
    - Give the pasta salad a final toss before serving. Taste and adjust seasoning if needed.
    - Serve chilled, garnished with additional parsley or basil if desired.

Tips:

- You can add grilled chicken, shrimp, or tofu to make it a complete meal.
- Feel free to customize the pasta salad with your favorite vegetables and cheeses.
- This pasta salad can be made ahead of time and stored in the refrigerator for up to 3 days.

Pasta salad is a crowd-pleaser and a great way to enjoy a variety of fresh vegetables with pasta. It's a perfect dish for kids to help assemble and enjoy as a side or main dish!

Stuffed peppers

Ingredients:

- 4 large bell peppers (any color)
- 1 lb ground beef or turkey (or use cooked quinoa for a vegetarian option)
- 1 small onion, finely chopped
- 2 cloves garlic, minced
- 1 cup cooked rice (white or brown)
- 1 cup tomato sauce or marinara sauce
- 1 teaspoon dried oregano
- 1 teaspoon dried basil
- Salt and pepper, to taste
- 1 cup shredded cheese (such as cheddar or mozzarella), divided

Instructions:

1. **Prepare the peppers:**
    - Preheat your oven to 375°F (190°C).
    - Cut the tops off the bell peppers and remove the seeds and membranes. You can also slice a thin layer off the bottom of each pepper if they don't stand upright on their own.
2. **Cook the filling:**
    - In a large skillet, cook the ground beef or turkey over medium-high heat until browned. If using quinoa, add it directly to the skillet.
    - Add the chopped onion and minced garlic to the skillet. Cook for 2-3 minutes until the onion is softened.
3. **Add rice and seasonings:**
    - Stir in the cooked rice (white or brown), tomato sauce or marinara sauce, dried oregano, dried basil, salt, and pepper. Cook for another 2-3 minutes until everything is heated through and well combined.
    - If the mixture seems too dry, you can add a splash of water or broth to moisten it slightly.
4. **Stuff the peppers:**
    - Place the hollowed-out bell peppers upright in a baking dish.
    - Spoon the filling mixture evenly into each pepper, packing it down gently.
5. **Bake the stuffed peppers:**
    - Cover the baking dish with aluminum foil and bake in the preheated oven for 30-35 minutes, or until the peppers are tender.
6. **Add cheese (optional):**
    - Remove the foil from the baking dish and sprinkle the tops of the stuffed peppers with shredded cheese.
    - Return the peppers to the oven and bake, uncovered, for an additional 5-10 minutes, or until the cheese is melted and bubbly.
7. **Serve:**

- Remove the stuffed peppers from the oven and let them cool for a few minutes before serving.
- Garnish with chopped fresh herbs like parsley or basil if desired.

Tips:

- You can customize the filling by adding other vegetables like diced tomatoes, corn, or spinach.
- Encourage kids to help with stuffing the peppers and sprinkling cheese on top.
- Leftover stuffed peppers can be stored in an airtight container in the refrigerator for up to 3 days.

Stuffed peppers are a wholesome and satisfying meal that's sure to please the whole family. Enjoy making and eating these delicious stuffed peppers together!

Rice crispy treats

Ingredients:

- 6 cups Rice Krispies cereal
- 4 cups mini marshmallows (or 1 bag of regular marshmallows)
- 3 tablespoons butter or margarine

Instructions:

1. **Prepare the pan:**
   - Grease a 9x13-inch baking pan with butter or cooking spray. Set aside.
2. **Melt the butter and marshmallows:**
   - In a large pot or saucepan, melt the butter over low heat.
   - Add the marshmallows and stir continuously until they are completely melted and smooth. Remove from heat.
3. **Mix in the cereal:**
   - Add the Rice Krispies cereal to the melted marshmallow mixture. Stir quickly until the cereal is evenly coated with marshmallow.
4. **Press into the pan:**
   - Using a buttered spatula or wax paper, press the mixture evenly into the prepared baking pan. Press down firmly to compact the mixture.
5. **Cool and cut:**
   - Let the Rice Krispies Treats cool at room temperature for about 30 minutes, or until set.
   - Once cooled and set, cut into squares or rectangles using a buttered knife or cookie cutter.
6. **Serve:**
   - Serve the Rice Krispies Treats squares immediately, or store them in an airtight container at room temperature for up to a few days.

Tips:

- For variations, you can add extras like chocolate chips, M&M's, nuts, or sprinkles to the mixture before pressing it into the pan.
- You can also drizzle melted chocolate over the cooled treats for extra flavor.
- If using regular marshmallows instead of mini marshmallows, increase the amount to 6 cups and melt them gradually with the butter over low heat.

Rice Krispies Treats are a delightful snack that's quick to make and perfect for kids to help with. Enjoy making and sharing these crispy, gooey treats!

Banana bread

Ingredients:

- 3 ripe bananas, mashed (about 1 1/2 cups)
- 1/3 cup unsalted butter, melted
- 3/4 cup granulated sugar
- 1 large egg, beaten
- 1 teaspoon vanilla extract
- 1 teaspoon baking soda
- Pinch of salt
- 1 1/2 cups all-purpose flour

Optional add-ins:

- 1/2 cup chopped nuts (such as walnuts or pecans)
- 1/2 cup chocolate chips
- 1/2 cup dried fruit (such as raisins or cranberries)

Instructions:

1. **Preheat oven and prepare pan:**
   - Preheat your oven to 350°F (175°C). Grease a 9x5-inch loaf pan or line it with parchment paper.
2. **Mix wet ingredients:**
   - In a mixing bowl, mash the ripe bananas with a fork or potato masher until smooth.
   - Stir in the melted butter, granulated sugar, beaten egg, and vanilla extract until well combined.
3. **Combine dry ingredients:**
   - Sprinkle the baking soda and salt over the banana mixture and gently stir.
   - Gradually add the flour to the bowl, stirring just until the flour is incorporated. Be careful not to overmix, as this can make the bread tough.
4. **Add optional add-ins:**
   - If using nuts, chocolate chips, or dried fruit, gently fold them into the batter until evenly distributed.
5. **Bake:**
   - Pour the batter into the prepared loaf pan, spreading it out evenly.
   - Bake in the preheated oven for 60-65 minutes, or until a toothpick inserted into the center of the bread comes out clean.
6. **Cool and serve:**
   - Allow the banana bread to cool in the pan for about 10 minutes, then transfer it to a wire rack to cool completely before slicing.

Tips:

- If your bananas aren't ripe enough, you can ripen them quickly by placing them in a paper bag with an apple or banana overnight.
- Feel free to customize the recipe by adding your favorite mix-ins, like cinnamon, nutmeg, or shredded coconut.
- Banana bread can be stored at room temperature in an airtight container for up to 3 days, or you can freeze it for longer storage.

Enjoy this homemade banana bread warm or at room temperature, as a delightful treat for breakfast or a snack any time of day!

Fruit salad

Ingredients:

- 2 cups strawberries, hulled and quartered
- 1 cup blueberries
- 1 cup grapes, halved
- 2 kiwis, peeled and diced
- 1 mango, peeled and diced
- 1 banana, sliced
- 1 orange, peeled and segmented
- 1 tablespoon honey (optional, for dressing)
- Juice of 1 lime or lemon (optional, for dressing)
- Fresh mint leaves, chopped (optional, for garnish)

Instructions:

1. **Prepare the fruits:**
   - Wash and prepare all the fruits as needed (hull strawberries, peel and dice mango and kiwis, halve grapes, etc.). Cut them into bite-sized pieces and place them in a large mixing bowl.
2. **Make the dressing (optional):**
   - In a small bowl, whisk together the honey and lime or lemon juice to make a simple dressing. This step is optional but adds a nice touch of sweetness and acidity to the fruit salad.
3. **Assemble the fruit salad:**
   - Pour the dressing over the prepared fruits in the mixing bowl. Gently toss the fruits together until they are evenly coated with the dressing.
4. **Chill (optional):**
   - Cover the bowl with plastic wrap or transfer the fruit salad to a serving dish. Refrigerate for at least 30 minutes to allow the flavors to meld together and the salad to chill.
5. **Serve:**
   - Before serving, garnish the fruit salad with fresh chopped mint leaves if desired. Serve chilled and enjoy!

Tips:

- Feel free to customize the fruit salad with your favorite fruits or whatever is in season.
- Add a sprinkle of toasted coconut or chopped nuts for extra texture and flavor.
- If making ahead, add the banana slices just before serving to prevent them from turning brown.

Fruit salad is not only delicious but also nutritious, providing a variety of vitamins, minerals, and antioxidants. It's a wonderful way to enjoy fresh fruits and is sure to be a hit with everyone, including kids!

Muffins (blueberry, banana, etc.)

Basic Muffin Recipe:

Ingredients:

- 2 cups all-purpose flour
- 1/2 cup granulated sugar
- 2 teaspoons baking powder
- 1/2 teaspoon baking soda
- 1/4 teaspoon salt
- 1 cup milk (whole milk or buttermilk preferred)
- 1/2 cup unsalted butter, melted and cooled slightly
- 1 large egg
- 1 teaspoon vanilla extract

For Blueberry Muffins:

- 1 cup fresh or frozen blueberries (if using frozen, do not thaw)

For Banana Muffins:

- 1 cup mashed ripe bananas (about 2 medium bananas)

Instructions:

1. **Preheat oven and prepare muffin tin:**
   - Preheat your oven to 375°F (190°C). Line a 12 cup muffin tin with paper liners or grease each cup lightly with butter or cooking spray.
2. **Mix dry ingredients:**
   - In a large bowl, whisk together the flour, sugar, baking powder, baking soda, and salt until well combined.
3. **Prepare wet ingredients:**
   - In another bowl, whisk together the milk, melted butter, egg, and vanilla extract until smooth.
4. **Combine wet and dry ingredients:**
   - Pour the wet ingredients into the bowl with the dry ingredients. Stir gently with a wooden spoon or rubber spatula until just combined. Do not overmix; the batter should be lumpy.
5. **Add fruit or other additions:**
   - **For Blueberry Muffins:** Gently fold in the blueberries into the batter until evenly distributed.
   - **For Banana Muffins:** Fold in the mashed bananas into the batter until just combined.
6. **Fill muffin cups:**
   - Divide the batter evenly among the muffin cups, filling each about 3/4 full.

7. **Bake:**
   - Bake in the preheated oven for 18-20 minutes, or until the tops are golden and a toothpick inserted into the center of a muffin comes out clean.
8. **Cool and serve:**
   - Remove the muffin tin from the oven and let the muffins cool in the tin for 5 minutes. Then transfer them to a wire rack to cool completely.

Tips:

- **Variations:** You can customize this basic muffin recipe by adding chocolate chips, nuts, cinnamon, or other fruits like raspberries or diced apples.
- **Storage:** Muffins can be stored in an airtight container at room temperature for up to 3 days, or you can freeze them for longer storage.
- **Mix-ins:** For added texture, sprinkle coarse sugar on top of each muffin before baking.

These homemade muffins are perfect for breakfast, snacks, or a quick treat any time of day. Enjoy experimenting with different flavors and ingredients to create your favorite muffin variations!

Veggie wraps

Ingredients:

- Large whole wheat or spinach tortillas
- Hummus or your favorite spread (such as Greek yogurt, guacamole, or tzatziki)
- Assorted fresh vegetables, thinly sliced or shredded:
    - Carrots
    - Cucumbers
    - Bell peppers (any color)
    - Cherry tomatoes, halved
    - Avocado slices
    - Spinach or lettuce leaves
- Optional add-ons:
    - Sliced cheese (like cheddar or Swiss)
    - Cooked quinoa or brown rice
    - Sunflower seeds or nuts
    - Fresh herbs (such as basil or cilantro)

Instructions:

1. **Prepare the vegetables:**
    - Wash and slice all the vegetables thinly. You can also shred carrots or cucumbers for added texture.
2. **Spread the hummus:**
    - Lay a tortilla flat on a clean surface. Spread a generous layer of hummus or your chosen spread evenly over the tortilla, leaving a small border around the edges.
3. **Layer the vegetables:**
    - Arrange a variety of sliced vegetables and other add-ons on top of the hummus-covered tortilla. You can layer them in rows or scatter them evenly.
4. **Add optional toppings:**
    - If desired, sprinkle with sunflower seeds, nuts, or fresh herbs for extra flavor and crunch.
5. **Wrap it up:**
    - Fold the sides of the tortilla inward, then roll it up tightly from the bottom to create a snug wrap. Press gently to secure the filling.
6. **Slice and serve:**
    - Use a sharp knife to slice the wrap diagonally into halves or thirds. Serve immediately, or wrap tightly in foil or parchment paper for later.

Tips:

- **Customization:** Feel free to customize your veggie wraps with your favorite vegetables, spreads, and add-ons. They're versatile and can accommodate various dietary preferences.

- **Make-ahead:** Veggie wraps are great for meal prep. Assemble them ahead of time, wrap tightly, and store in the refrigerator until ready to eat.
- **Kids in the kitchen:** Let kids help with washing vegetables, spreading hummus, arranging fillings, and rolling up the wraps. It's a fun and interactive way to involve them in meal preparation.

Veggie wraps are a nutritious option for lunches, picnics, or anytime you want a quick and healthy meal. Enjoy the fresh flavors and textures in every bite!

Cheese and vegetable frittata

Ingredients:

- 6 large eggs
- 1/4 cup milk or half-and-half
- Salt and pepper, to taste
- 1 tablespoon olive oil or butter
- 1/2 small onion, diced
- 1 bell pepper (any color), diced
- 1 cup cherry tomatoes, halved
- 1 cup baby spinach leaves
- 1/2 cup shredded cheese (cheddar, mozzarella, or your favorite cheese)
- Fresh herbs for garnish (optional)

Instructions:

1. **Preheat oven:** Preheat your oven to 350°F (175°C).
2. **Prepare vegetables:** Heat olive oil or butter in an oven-safe skillet over medium heat. Add diced onion and bell pepper, sauté until softened, about 5 minutes.
3. **Add tomatoes and spinach:** Add cherry tomatoes to the skillet and cook for 1-2 minutes until they start to soften. Stir in baby spinach leaves and cook until wilted, about 1 minute. Season with salt and pepper to taste.
4. **Whisk eggs:** In a mixing bowl, whisk together eggs, milk or half-and-half, salt, and pepper until well combined.
5. **Combine eggs and vegetables:** Pour the egg mixture evenly over the sautéed vegetables in the skillet. Gently stir to distribute the vegetables throughout the eggs.
6. **Add cheese:** Sprinkle shredded cheese evenly over the top of the frittata.
7. **Bake:** Transfer the skillet to the preheated oven and bake for 15-20 minutes, or until the frittata is set in the center and the edges are golden brown.
8. **Finish and serve:** Remove the frittata from the oven and let it cool slightly. Garnish with fresh herbs if desired. Slice into wedges and serve warm.

Tips:

- **Variations:** Feel free to add other vegetables such as mushrooms, zucchini, or broccoli. You can also experiment with different cheeses or add cooked meats like ham or bacon.
- **Make-ahead:** Frittatas can be made ahead of time and stored in the refrigerator. They can be reheated gently in the oven or microwave before serving.
- **Serve with:** Frittatas are delicious on their own, but you can also serve them with a side salad, crusty bread, or fresh fruit for a complete meal.

This cheese and vegetable frittata is hearty, nutritious, and easy to customize based on your preferences. It's a great dish to enjoy with family and friends any time of day!

Bread rolls

Ingredients:

- 4 cups all-purpose flour
- 2 teaspoons instant yeast
- 2 tablespoons granulated sugar
- 1 teaspoon salt
- 1 cup warm milk (about 110°F or 45°C)
- 1/4 cup unsalted butter, melted
- 1 large egg

Instructions:

1. **Prepare the dough:**
    - In a large mixing bowl or the bowl of a stand mixer fitted with a dough hook attachment, combine 3 cups of flour, instant yeast, sugar, and salt.
    - In a separate bowl, whisk together the warm milk, melted butter, and egg.
    - Pour the wet ingredients into the dry ingredients. Mix until a soft dough forms. If the dough is too sticky, gradually add more flour, 1 tablespoon at a time, until the dough pulls away from the sides of the bowl.
2. **Knead the dough:**
    - Turn the dough out onto a lightly floured surface. Knead the dough for about 8-10 minutes until it is smooth and elastic. Alternatively, knead the dough in the stand mixer on medium speed for about 5-7 minutes.
3. **First rise:**
    - Place the dough in a greased bowl and cover it with a clean kitchen towel or plastic wrap. Let it rise in a warm, draft-free place for about 1-1.5 hours, or until doubled in size.
4. **Shape the rolls:**
    - Punch down the risen dough to release the air. Divide the dough into 12 equal pieces. Shape each piece into a smooth ball.
    - Place the shaped rolls onto a greased or parchment-lined baking sheet, spacing them a few inches apart.
5. **Second rise:**
    - Cover the rolls loosely with a kitchen towel and let them rise again for about 30-45 minutes, until puffy and nearly doubled in size.
6. **Bake:**
    - Preheat your oven to 375°F (190°C) while the rolls are rising.
    - Bake the rolls in the preheated oven for 15-18 minutes, or until they are golden brown on top and sound hollow when tapped.
7. **Cool and serve:**
    - Remove the rolls from the oven and let them cool on a wire rack for a few minutes before serving.

Tips:

- **Variations:** You can brush the tops of the rolls with melted butter or egg wash before baking for a shiny finish. You can also sprinkle them with sesame seeds, poppy seeds, or shredded cheese before baking for added flavor.
- **Storage:** Store leftover rolls in an airtight container at room temperature for up to 2 days. They can also be frozen for longer storage. Thaw at room temperature and reheat in the oven before serving.

Homemade bread rolls are perfect for sandwiches, alongside soups, or simply enjoyed warm with butter. They're a wonderful baking project that everyone in the family can enjoy!

Baked potato wedges

Ingredients:

- 4 large russet potatoes, scrubbed and dried
- 2-3 tablespoons olive oil
- 1 teaspoon garlic powder
- 1 teaspoon paprika
- 1/2 teaspoon dried thyme
- 1/2 teaspoon dried rosemary (optional)
- Salt and pepper, to taste

Instructions:

1. **Preheat oven:**
    - Preheat your oven to 425°F (220°C). Line a baking sheet with parchment paper or aluminum foil for easy cleanup.
2. **Prepare the potatoes:**
    - Cut each potato lengthwise into wedges. Aim for wedges that are about 1/2 to 3/4 inch thick. Try to keep them as uniform in size as possible for even baking.
3. **Season the wedges:**
    - In a large bowl, toss the potato wedges with olive oil until evenly coated.
    - Sprinkle garlic powder, paprika, dried thyme, dried rosemary (if using), salt, and pepper over the wedges. Toss again until the wedges are coated with the seasonings.
4. **Arrange on baking sheet:**
    - Arrange the seasoned potato wedges in a single layer on the prepared baking sheet, leaving space between each wedge to ensure even cooking.
5. **Bake:**
    - Bake in the preheated oven for 30-35 minutes, flipping halfway through, until the potato wedges are golden brown and crispy on the outside, and tender on the inside.
6. **Serve:**
    - Remove the baked potato wedges from the oven and let them cool slightly. Serve warm with your favorite dipping sauce, such as ketchup, aioli, or ranch dressing.

Tips:

- **Variations:** You can customize the seasonings to your preference. Try adding chili powder, cumin, Parmesan cheese, or fresh herbs like parsley or cilantro.
- **Crispiness:** For extra crispy potato wedges, after tossing them in olive oil and seasonings, place them on a wire rack set over the baking sheet. This allows hot air to circulate around the wedges, promoting even crisping.
- **Storage:** Leftover potato wedges can be stored in an airtight container in the refrigerator for 2-3 days. Reheat them in the oven or toaster oven to restore their crispiness.

Baked potato wedges are a healthier alternative to fried potatoes and make a delicious side dish or snack. They're simple to prepare and sure to be a hit with the whole family!

Sushi rolls

Ingredients:

- Sushi rice (2 cups)
- Nori sheets (seaweed sheets)
- Rice vinegar (2 tablespoons)
- Sugar (1 tablespoon)
- Salt (1/2 teaspoon)
- Assorted fillings:
    - Cucumber, thinly sliced into matchsticks
    - Avocado, sliced
    - Carrot, peeled and thinly sliced into matchsticks
    - Cooked shrimp, crab meat, or smoked salmon (optional)
- Soy sauce, pickled ginger, and wasabi (for serving)

Instructions:

1. **Prepare the sushi rice:**
    - Rinse the sushi rice under cold water until the water runs clear. Cook the rice according to package instructions or in a rice cooker.
    - In a small bowl, mix rice vinegar, sugar, and salt until dissolved. When the rice is cooked, transfer it to a large bowl and gently fold in the vinegar mixture using a rice paddle or wooden spoon. Allow the rice to cool to room temperature.
2. **Prepare the fillings:**
    - Prepare your fillings by slicing vegetables and seafood into thin strips or slices. Have them ready for assembly.
3. **Assemble the sushi rolls:**
    - Place a bamboo sushi rolling mat on a clean surface. Lay a sheet of nori, shiny side down, on the mat.
    - Wet your fingers with water to prevent sticking, then spread a thin layer of sushi rice evenly over the nori, leaving about 1 inch of the nori sheet uncovered at the top edge.
    - Arrange your desired fillings horizontally in the center of the rice-covered nori sheet.
4. **Roll the sushi:**
    - Lift the edge of the bamboo mat closest to you, and tightly roll the nori sheet and rice over the fillings, using the mat to shape and compress the roll as you go.
    - Once rolled, press gently on the bamboo mat to seal the roll. Moisten the exposed nori edge with a little water and press to seal.
5. **Slice and serve:**
    - Use a sharp knife dipped in water to slice the sushi roll into 6-8 pieces. Wipe the knife clean between cuts for cleaner slices.
    - Serve the sushi rolls with soy sauce, pickled ginger, and wasabi on the side.

Tips:

- **Variations:** You can customize your sushi rolls with different fillings like fish, tofu, or other vegetables like bell peppers or lettuce. Get creative with combinations that you enjoy!
- **Handling nori:** Keep nori sheets dry until ready to use to prevent them from becoming soggy.
- **Practice makes perfect:** Rolling sushi takes practice. Don't worry if your first rolls aren't perfect; they will still taste delicious!

Making sushi rolls at home allows you to experiment with flavors and ingredients while enjoying a traditional Japanese dish. Have fun and enjoy your homemade sushi rolls!

Grilled cheese sandwiches

Ingredients:

- 2 slices of bread (white bread, whole wheat, sourdough, or your choice)
- Butter or margarine, softened
- Cheese slices (cheddar, American, Swiss, mozzarella, or your favorite melting cheese)

Optional add-ins:

- Sliced tomatoes
- Cooked bacon or ham
- Avocado slices
- Caramelized onions
- Spinach leaves

Instructions:

1. **Preheat a skillet or griddle:**
    - Heat a non-stick skillet or griddle over medium heat.
2. **Butter the bread:**
    - Spread one side of each slice of bread with butter or margarine.
3. **Assemble the sandwich:**
    - Place one slice of bread, buttered side down, on the skillet or griddle.
    - Layer cheese slices (and any optional add-ins) on top of the bread.
    - Top with the second slice of bread, buttered side facing up.
4. **Grill the sandwich:**
    - Cook the sandwich for 3-4 minutes on each side, or until the bread is golden brown and the cheese is melted.
    - If desired, press down gently on the sandwich with a spatula to flatten slightly while grilling.
5. **Serve:**
    - Remove the grilled cheese sandwich from the skillet or griddle and let it cool for a minute or two.
    - Cut the sandwich diagonally into halves or quarters, if desired, and serve hot.

Tips:

- **Variations:** Experiment with different types of bread and cheeses to create unique flavors. Adding vegetables or meats can also enhance the sandwich.
- **Cooking tips:** Lower the heat if the bread is browning too quickly before the cheese melts. Covering the skillet with a lid while cooking can help the cheese melt faster.
- **Serving suggestions:** Grilled cheese sandwiches pair well with tomato soup, a side salad, or pickles.

Grilled cheese sandwiches are quick to prepare and perfect for a comforting lunch or dinner option. They're versatile, allowing you to customize them to suit your taste preferences. Enjoy making and savoring these cheesy delights!

Chicken skewers

Ingredients:

- 1.5 lbs (about 700g) boneless, skinless chicken breasts or thighs, cut into 1-inch cubes
- 2 tablespoons olive oil
- 2 cloves garlic, minced
- 1 teaspoon paprika
- 1/2 teaspoon ground cumin
- 1/2 teaspoon ground coriander
- 1/2 teaspoon salt
- 1/4 teaspoon black pepper
- Juice of 1 lemon
- Wooden or metal skewers (if using wooden skewers, soak them in water for 30 minutes to prevent burning)

Instructions:

1. **Prepare the marinade:**
   - In a bowl, combine olive oil, minced garlic, paprika, cumin, coriander, salt, pepper, and lemon juice. Mix well to combine.
2. **Marinate the chicken:**
   - Place the chicken cubes in a large resealable plastic bag or shallow dish. Pour the marinade over the chicken, making sure all pieces are evenly coated. Marinate in the refrigerator for at least 30 minutes, or up to 4 hours for maximum flavor.
3. **Assemble the skewers:**
   - If using wooden skewers, thread the marinated chicken pieces onto the skewers, leaving a small space between each piece. Metal skewers can be used directly.
4. **Grill the skewers:**
   - Preheat your grill to medium-high heat or preheat a grill pan over medium-high heat on the stovetop.
   - Lightly oil the grill grates or grill pan to prevent sticking.
   - Place the chicken skewers on the grill and cook for 5-7 minutes per side, or until the chicken is fully cooked through and has nice grill marks. Turn occasionally to ensure even cooking.
5. **Serve:**
   - Remove the chicken skewers from the grill and let them rest for a few minutes before serving.
   - Serve hot with your favorite sides, such as rice, salad, or grilled vegetables.

Tips:

- **Variations:** You can add vegetables like bell peppers, onions, or cherry tomatoes between the chicken pieces on the skewers for added flavor and color.

- **Cooking methods:** If you don't have a grill, you can bake the skewers in the oven at 400°F (200°C) for about 20-25 minutes, turning once halfway through cooking.
- **Safety:** Ensure chicken is cooked to an internal temperature of 165°F (75°C) to be safe for consumption.

Chicken skewers are a versatile dish that's great for a main course at a barbecue, as a party appetizer, or served with rice for a complete meal. Enjoy the delicious flavors of these tender and juicy chicken skewers!

Oatmeal cookies

Ingredients:

- 1 cup unsalted butter, softened
- 1 cup packed brown sugar
- 1/2 cup granulated sugar
- 2 large eggs
- 1 teaspoon vanilla extract
- 1 1/2 cups all-purpose flour
- 1 teaspoon baking soda
- 1 teaspoon ground cinnamon
- 1/2 teaspoon salt
- 3 cups old-fashioned rolled oats
- 1 cup raisins, chocolate chips, or chopped nuts (optional)

Instructions:

1. **Preheat oven:**
   - Preheat your oven to 350°F (175°C). Line baking sheets with parchment paper or silicone baking mats.
2. **Cream butter and sugars:**
   - In a large bowl, cream together the softened butter, brown sugar, and granulated sugar until light and fluffy.
3. **Add eggs and vanilla:**
   - Beat in the eggs one at a time, then add the vanilla extract, mixing until well combined.
4. **Combine dry ingredients:**
   - In a separate bowl, whisk together the flour, baking soda, cinnamon, and salt.
5. **Mix wet and dry ingredients:**
   - Gradually add the dry ingredients to the wet ingredients, mixing until just combined.
6. **Add oats and optional ingredients:**
   - Stir in the rolled oats and your choice of raisins, chocolate chips, or nuts until evenly distributed in the dough.
7. **Form dough balls:**
   - Drop rounded tablespoons of dough onto the prepared baking sheets, spacing them about 2 inches apart.
8. **Bake:**
   - Bake in the preheated oven for 10-12 minutes, or until the edges are golden brown.
9. **Cool and store:**
   - Allow the cookies to cool on the baking sheets for a few minutes before transferring them to wire racks to cool completely.

Tips:

- **Variations:** You can customize your oatmeal cookies by adding dried cranberries, chopped dates, shredded coconut, or even a touch of nutmeg or cloves for extra flavor.
- **Storage:** Store cooled cookies in an airtight container at room temperature for up to one week. They can also be frozen for longer storage.
- **Soft vs. crispy:** For softer cookies, bake for slightly less time. For crispier cookies, bake for a few minutes longer.

These oatmeal cookies are chewy, flavorful, and perfect for sharing with family and friends. Enjoy them with a glass of milk or a cup of tea for a delightful treat!

Mini meatloaves

Ingredients:

- 1 lb ground beef (you can also use a mix of ground beef and ground pork)
- 1/2 cup breadcrumbs
- 1/4 cup milk
- 1 small onion, finely chopped
- 1 garlic clove, minced
- 1/4 cup grated Parmesan cheese (optional)
- 1 large egg, lightly beaten
- 2 tablespoons ketchup
- 1 tablespoon Worcestershire sauce
- 1 teaspoon dried oregano
- 1/2 teaspoon salt
- 1/4 teaspoon black pepper
- Fresh parsley, chopped (for garnish, optional)

Glaze:

- 1/4 cup ketchup
- 1 tablespoon brown sugar
- 1 teaspoon Dijon mustard

Instructions:

1. **Preheat oven:**
   - Preheat your oven to 375°F (190°C). Line a baking sheet with parchment paper or foil for easy cleanup.
2. **Prepare meatloaf mixture:**
   - In a large bowl, combine ground beef, breadcrumbs, milk, chopped onion, minced garlic, Parmesan cheese (if using), beaten egg, ketchup, Worcestershire sauce, dried oregano, salt, and pepper. Mix gently until well combined.
3. **Shape mini meatloaves:**
   - Divide the meat mixture into 6 equal portions. Shape each portion into a mini loaf shape and place them on the prepared baking sheet.
4. **Prepare the glaze:**
   - In a small bowl, mix together ketchup, brown sugar, and Dijon mustard until smooth. Brush or spoon the glaze over the tops of the mini meatloaves.
5. **Bake:**
   - Bake in the preheated oven for 25-30 minutes, or until the meatloaves are cooked through and the internal temperature reaches 160°F (71°C).
6. **Serve:**
   - Remove the mini meatloaves from the oven and let them rest for a few minutes before serving. Sprinkle with chopped parsley for garnish if desired.

Tips:

- **Variations:** You can customize your mini meatloaves by adding diced bell peppers, carrots, or mushrooms to the meat mixture for added flavor and texture.
- **Storage:** Leftover mini meatloaves can be stored in an airtight container in the refrigerator for up to 3 days. They can also be frozen for up to 3 months. Thaw overnight in the refrigerator before reheating.
- **Serving suggestions:** Serve mini meatloaves with mashed potatoes, steamed vegetables, or a side salad for a complete meal.

These mini meatloaves are hearty, flavorful, and perfect for a family dinner or meal prep. Enjoy the comforting flavors of meatloaf in individual portions!

Veggie burgers

Ingredients:

- 1 can (15 oz) black beans, drained and rinsed
- 1 cup cooked quinoa or brown rice
- 1/2 cup breadcrumbs (use gluten-free breadcrumbs if needed)
- 1/2 cup finely chopped onion
- 1/2 cup grated carrot
- 1/4 cup chopped fresh cilantro or parsley
- 2 cloves garlic, minced
- 1 tablespoon soy sauce or tamari (for gluten-free option)
- 1 teaspoon ground cumin
- 1/2 teaspoon paprika
- Salt and pepper, to taste
- 1 tablespoon olive oil, for cooking

Optional toppings and serving suggestions:

- Burger buns (whole wheat, gluten-free, or your choice)
- Lettuce leaves
- Sliced tomatoes
- Avocado slices
- Red onion slices
- Pickles
- Mustard, ketchup, or your favorite burger sauce

Instructions:

1. **Prepare the veggie burger mixture:**
   - In a large bowl, mash the black beans with a fork or potato masher until mostly smooth, leaving some chunks for texture.
   - Add cooked quinoa or brown rice, breadcrumbs, chopped onion, grated carrot, cilantro or parsley, minced garlic, soy sauce or tamari, ground cumin, paprika, salt, and pepper to the mashed beans. Mix until well combined.
2. **Form the patties:**
   - Divide the mixture into 4 equal portions. Shape each portion into a patty about 1/2-inch thick. If the mixture is too wet to handle, add a little more breadcrumbs.
3. **Cook the veggie burgers:**
   - Heat olive oil in a large skillet over medium heat. Place the patties in the skillet and cook for 4-5 minutes on each side, or until golden brown and heated through.
   - Alternatively, you can bake the veggie burgers. Preheat your oven to 375°F (190°C). Place the patties on a lightly greased baking sheet and bake for 15-20 minutes, flipping halfway through.
4. **Assemble the veggie burgers:**

- Toast the burger buns if desired. Place a veggie burger patty on the bottom half of each bun.
- Add your favorite toppings such as lettuce, tomato slices, avocado, red onion, pickles, and sauces.

5. **Serve:**
   - Serve the veggie burgers immediately while warm.

Tips:

- **Make ahead:** You can prepare the veggie burger mixture ahead of time and refrigerate it for up to 2 days before cooking. This allows the flavors to meld together.
- **Freezing:** Cooked veggie burger patties can be frozen for up to 3 months. Wrap each patty individually in plastic wrap and store them in a freezer-safe container. Thaw overnight in the refrigerator before reheating.
- **Customization:** Feel free to customize the veggie burgers by adding other vegetables like bell peppers, mushrooms, or spinach. You can also experiment with different seasonings and herbs to suit your taste preferences.

These homemade veggie burgers are packed with flavor and wholesome ingredients, making them a satisfying and healthy alternative to traditional meat burgers. Enjoy creating and savoring these delicious burgers!

Berry crumble

Ingredients:

For the filling:

- 4 cups mixed berries (such as strawberries, blueberries, raspberries, blackberries)
- 1/4 cup granulated sugar (adjust depending on the sweetness of the berries)
- 1 tablespoon cornstarch
- 1 tablespoon fresh lemon juice
- Zest of 1 lemon (optional)

For the crumble topping:

- 1 cup old-fashioned rolled oats
- 1/2 cup all-purpose flour
- 1/2 cup packed brown sugar
- 1/2 teaspoon ground cinnamon
- 1/4 teaspoon salt
- 1/2 cup (1 stick) unsalted butter, cold and cut into small cubes

Instructions:

1. **Preheat oven:**
   - Preheat your oven to 350°F (175°C). Grease a 9-inch square baking dish or a similar-sized baking dish with butter or cooking spray.
2. **Prepare the berry filling:**
   - In a large bowl, gently toss together the mixed berries, granulated sugar, cornstarch, lemon juice, and lemon zest (if using). Make sure the berries are evenly coated.
3. **Make the crumble topping:**
   - In another bowl, combine the rolled oats, flour, brown sugar, ground cinnamon, and salt. Mix well.
   - Add the cold cubed butter to the oat mixture. Using your fingertips or a pastry cutter, work the butter into the dry ingredients until the mixture resembles coarse crumbs and the butter is well incorporated.
4. **Assemble and bake:**
   - Spread the berry mixture evenly in the prepared baking dish.
   - Sprinkle the crumble topping evenly over the berries, covering them completely.
5. **Bake the crumble:**
   - Place the baking dish in the preheated oven and bake for 35-40 minutes, or until the berry filling is bubbling and the crumble topping is golden brown and crispy.
6. **Serve:**
   - Remove the berry crumble from the oven and let it cool slightly before serving.
   - Serve warm with a scoop of vanilla ice cream or a dollop of whipped cream, if desired.

Tips:

- **Variations:** You can personalize your berry crumble by using different combinations of berries or adding a handful of chopped nuts (such as almonds or pecans) to the crumble topping for extra crunch.
- **Storage:** Leftover berry crumble can be stored in the refrigerator, covered, for up to 3 days. Reheat in the oven or microwave before serving.
- **Gluten-free option:** Substitute gluten-free flour and certified gluten-free oats to make this dessert gluten-free.

Berry crumble is a comforting and versatile dessert that can be enjoyed year-round, especially when berries are in season. It's perfect for gatherings or simply as a special treat after a meal. Enjoy the sweet and tangy flavors of this delicious dessert!

Tortilla chips and guacamole

Homemade Guacamole Recipe:

Ingredients:

- 3 ripe avocados
- 1 lime, juiced
- 1/2 teaspoon salt, or more to taste
- 1/2 teaspoon ground cumin
- 1/4 teaspoon cayenne pepper (optional, for a spicy kick)
- 1/2 cup diced red onion
- 1 large tomato, diced
- 1/4 cup chopped fresh cilantro
- 1-2 cloves garlic, minced

Instructions:

1. **Prepare the avocados:**
   - Cut the avocados in half lengthwise, remove the pits, and scoop the flesh into a medium-sized bowl.
2. **Mash the avocados:**
   - Mash the avocados with a fork or potato masher until you reach your desired consistency (smooth or chunky).
3. **Season the guacamole:**
   - Squeeze the lime juice over the mashed avocados. Add salt, ground cumin, and cayenne pepper (if using). Mix well to combine.
4. **Add vegetables and herbs:**
   - Stir in the diced red onion, diced tomato, chopped cilantro, and minced garlic. Mix until all ingredients are evenly distributed.
5. **Adjust seasoning:**
   - Taste the guacamole and adjust seasoning as needed, adding more salt or lime juice if desired.
6. **Serve:**
   - Transfer the guacamole to a serving bowl.

Serving Tortilla Chips and Guacamole:

- **Choose your tortilla chips:** You can use store-bought tortilla chips or make your own by cutting corn tortillas into triangles, brushing them with olive oil, and baking them until crispy.
- **Arrange and enjoy:** Place a bowl of freshly made guacamole alongside a bowl of tortilla chips. Garnish the guacamole with extra cilantro, diced tomatoes, or a sprinkle of paprika for added flavor and presentation.
- **Storage:** Guacamole is best served fresh but can be stored in an airtight container with plastic wrap pressed directly onto the surface of the guacamole (to prevent browning) for up to one day in the refrigerator.

- **Variations:** Feel free to customize your guacamole by adding ingredients like diced jalapeño for heat, mango or pineapple for sweetness, or crumbled queso fresco for extra creaminess.

Tortilla chips and guacamole are a delicious combination that's perfect for parties, game nights, or simply as a tasty snack. Enjoy the creamy texture of the guacamole paired with the satisfying crunch of the tortilla chips!

Ratatouille

Ingredients:

- 1 large eggplant, diced
- 2 zucchinis, diced
- 1 red bell pepper, diced
- 1 yellow bell pepper, diced
- 1 onion, diced
- 3-4 cloves garlic, minced
- 4 tomatoes, diced (or 1 can of diced tomatoes)
- 2 tablespoons tomato paste
- 1/4 cup olive oil
- 1 teaspoon dried thyme
- 1 teaspoon dried oregano
- Salt and pepper, to taste
- Fresh basil or parsley, chopped (for garnish)

Instructions:

1. **Prepare the vegetables:**
   - Dice the eggplant, zucchinis, red and yellow bell peppers, onion, and tomatoes into evenly sized pieces.
2. **Sauté the vegetables:**
   - In a large skillet or Dutch oven, heat the olive oil over medium heat. Add the diced onion and cook until translucent, about 5 minutes.
   - Add the minced garlic and cook for another minute until fragrant.
   - Add the diced eggplant to the skillet and cook for 5-7 minutes, stirring occasionally, until it starts to soften.
   - Add the diced zucchini, red and yellow bell peppers to the skillet. Cook for an additional 5 minutes, stirring occasionally.
3. **Simmer the ratatouille:**
   - Stir in the diced tomatoes, tomato paste, dried thyme, dried oregano, salt, and pepper. Mix well to combine.
   - Reduce the heat to low, cover the skillet, and let the ratatouille simmer for 20-25 minutes, stirring occasionally, until all the vegetables are tender and flavors have melded together.
4. **Adjust seasoning and serve:**
   - Taste the ratatouille and adjust seasoning with more salt and pepper if needed.
   - Garnish with chopped fresh basil or parsley before serving.
5. **Serve:**
   - Ratatouille can be served hot, warm, or at room temperature. It's delicious on its own or as a side dish with crusty bread, pasta, rice, or grilled meats.

Tips:

- **Variations:** Ratatouille is quite forgiving and adaptable. You can add other vegetables such as mushrooms, celery, or even chickpeas for added protein.

- **Storage:** Ratatouille tastes even better the next day as the flavors continue to meld. Store leftovers in an airtight container in the refrigerator for up to 4 days.
- **Freezing:** Ratatouille freezes well. Let it cool completely, then transfer to freezer-safe containers or bags. Freeze for up to 3 months. Thaw overnight in the refrigerator before reheating.

Ratatouille is a delicious way to enjoy the bounty of summer vegetables. It's hearty, flavorful, and makes for a satisfying meal that's also healthy and nutritious. Enjoy this classic French dish as a versatile addition to your culinary repertoire!

Breaded fish fillets

Ingredients:

- 4 fish fillets (such as tilapia, cod, haddock, or any white fish)
- 1 cup breadcrumbs (plain or seasoned)
- 1/2 cup all-purpose flour
- 2 eggs, beaten
- 1/2 teaspoon salt
- 1/4 teaspoon black pepper
- 1/4 teaspoon paprika (optional)
- Vegetable oil, for frying
- Lemon wedges, for serving
- Tartar sauce or your favorite dipping sauce, for serving

Instructions:

1. **Prepare the breading station:**
    - Set up three shallow bowls or plates. Place flour in one bowl, beaten eggs in another bowl, and breadcrumbs mixed with salt, pepper, and paprika (if using) in the third bowl.
2. **Bread the fish fillets:**
    - Pat the fish fillets dry with paper towels to remove excess moisture.
    - Dredge each fish fillet in the flour, shaking off any excess.
    - Dip the floured fish fillet into the beaten eggs, ensuring it's coated evenly.
    - Press the fish fillet into the breadcrumb mixture, coating both sides thoroughly. Press gently to adhere the breadcrumbs.
3. **Fry the breaded fish fillets:**
    - In a large skillet, heat enough vegetable oil over medium-high heat to cover the bottom of the skillet.
    - Carefully place the breaded fish fillets into the hot oil, making sure not to overcrowd the pan. Cook in batches if necessary.
    - Fry the fish fillets for about 3-4 minutes on each side, or until the breading is golden brown and crispy and the fish is cooked through. The internal temperature of the fish should reach 145°F (63°C).
4. **Serve:**
    - Remove the breaded fish fillets from the skillet and place them on a plate lined with paper towels to absorb any excess oil.
    - Serve the breaded fish fillets hot, garnished with lemon wedges and accompanied by tartar sauce or your favorite dipping sauce.

Tips:

- **Oven-baking option:** For a healthier alternative, you can bake the breaded fish fillets in a preheated oven at 400°F (200°C) for 15-20 minutes, or until golden and cooked through.

- **Variations:** Experiment with different types of breadcrumbs or add herbs like chopped parsley or dill to the breadcrumb mixture for extra flavor.
- **Serving suggestions:** Breaded fish fillets are delicious served with coleslaw, steamed vegetables, or a side salad. They also make great fish sandwiches on toasted buns.

Homemade breaded fish fillets are crispy on the outside and tender on the inside, making them a family-friendly meal that's sure to please. Enjoy this easy and tasty recipe!

Rice pudding

Ingredients:

- 1/2 cup long-grain white rice
- 4 cups whole milk
- 1/2 cup granulated sugar
- 1/4 teaspoon salt
- 1 teaspoon vanilla extract
- 1/2 teaspoon ground cinnamon
- 1/4 teaspoon ground nutmeg
- Optional toppings: raisins, chopped nuts, or fresh berries

Instructions:

1. **Rinse and cook the rice:**
   - Rinse the rice under cold water until the water runs clear to remove excess starch.
   - In a medium saucepan, combine the rinsed rice and 2 cups of water. Bring to a boil over medium-high heat. Reduce the heat to low, cover, and simmer for 15-20 minutes, or until the rice is tender and the water is absorbed.
2. **Make the rice pudding:**
   - Stir in the milk, sugar, and salt into the cooked rice in the saucepan.
   - Cook over medium heat, stirring frequently, until the mixture comes to a simmer.
3. **Simmer and thicken:**
   - Reduce the heat to low and simmer gently, stirring occasionally, for about 30-40 minutes, or until the mixture thickens to a creamy consistency. Stir more frequently towards the end of cooking to prevent sticking.
4. **Add flavorings:**
   - Stir in the vanilla extract, ground cinnamon, and ground nutmeg. Adjust the sweetness and spices to taste.
5. **Cool and serve:**
   - Remove the rice pudding from heat and let it cool slightly.
   - Serve warm or chilled, garnished with a sprinkle of ground cinnamon or your choice of toppings such as raisins, chopped nuts, or fresh berries.

Tips:

- **Storage:** Store any leftover rice pudding in an airtight container in the refrigerator for up to 3-4 days. It can be enjoyed cold or reheated gently on the stove or in the microwave.
- **Variations:** You can customize your rice pudding by adding different flavors such as cardamom, orange zest, or almond extract. You can also experiment with different types of milk (such as coconut milk or almond milk) for a dairy-free version.
- **Creamier texture:** For an even creamier texture, you can stir in a beaten egg yolk towards the end of cooking. Make sure to temper the egg yolk with a small amount of the hot rice pudding mixture before adding it to the saucepan.

Rice pudding is a versatile dessert that can be enjoyed warm or cold, and it's perfect for any occasion. Its rich, comforting flavors make it a favorite dessert in many households. Enjoy making and savoring this homemade treat!

Stuffed mushrooms

Ingredients:

- 16 large white or cremini mushrooms
- 1/2 cup breadcrumbs (plain or seasoned)
- 1/4 cup grated Parmesan cheese
- 2 tablespoons olive oil
- 2 cloves garlic, minced
- 2 tablespoons fresh parsley, chopped
- Salt and pepper, to taste
- Optional: 1/4 cup finely chopped onions or shallots, 1/4 cup diced bell peppers, 1/4 cup cooked and crumbled sausage or bacon

Instructions:

1. **Prepare the mushrooms:**
   - Preheat your oven to 375°F (190°C). Line a baking sheet with parchment paper for easy cleanup.
   - Remove the stems from the mushrooms and finely chop them. Set the mushroom caps aside.
2. **Prepare the filling:**
   - In a skillet, heat 1 tablespoon of olive oil over medium heat. Add the chopped mushroom stems (and optional onions/shallots, bell peppers if using) and cook for 3-4 minutes until softened.
   - Add the minced garlic and cook for another 1-2 minutes until fragrant.
   - Remove from heat and transfer the cooked mushroom mixture to a bowl.
3. **Make the stuffing mixture:**
   - To the bowl with the cooked mushroom mixture, add breadcrumbs, grated Parmesan cheese, chopped parsley, remaining 1 tablespoon of olive oil, salt, and pepper. Mix well to combine. Adjust seasoning to taste.
4. **Stuff the mushrooms:**
   - Spoon the filling mixture generously into each mushroom cap, pressing lightly to pack it in.
5. **Bake the stuffed mushrooms:**
   - Place the stuffed mushrooms on the prepared baking sheet.
   - Bake in the preheated oven for 18-20 minutes, or until the mushrooms are tender and the filling is golden brown on top.
6. **Serve:**
   - Remove from the oven and let the stuffed mushrooms cool slightly before serving.
   - Garnish with additional chopped parsley if desired.

Tips:

- **Variations:** Feel free to customize the stuffing mixture by adding ingredients like cooked and crumbled sausage or bacon, chopped spinach, sun-dried tomatoes, or different types of cheese.

- **Make-ahead:** You can prepare the stuffed mushrooms ahead of time and refrigerate them before baking. Bake them just before serving for best results.
- **Serve warm:** Stuffed mushrooms are best served warm. They make a great appetizer for parties or a flavorful side dish for any meal.

These stuffed mushrooms are savory, flavorful, and make for an impressive appetizer. Enjoy making and sharing them with family and friends!

Garlic bread

Ingredients:

- 1 loaf of Italian bread or French baguette
- 1/2 cup (1 stick) unsalted butter, softened
- 4 cloves garlic, minced
- 2 tablespoons fresh parsley, finely chopped (optional)
- Salt, to taste
- Pepper, to taste
- 1/2 cup grated Parmesan cheese (optional)

Instructions:

1. **Preheat the oven:** Preheat your oven to 375°F (190°C).
2. **Prepare the garlic butter:**
   - In a small bowl, mix together the softened butter, minced garlic, chopped parsley (if using), salt, and pepper. Add grated Parmesan cheese if desired for extra flavor.
3. **Prepare the bread:**
   - Slice the loaf of Italian bread or French baguette in half lengthwise, creating two long halves.
4. **Spread the garlic butter:**
   - Spread the garlic butter mixture evenly over the cut sides of the bread halves. Make sure to spread it all the way to the edges for even flavor.
5. **Assemble and bake:**
   - Place the garlic bread halves, buttered side up, on a baking sheet lined with parchment paper or aluminum foil for easy cleanup.
6. **Bake the garlic bread:**
   - Bake in the preheated oven for 10-12 minutes, or until the edges are golden brown and the butter is melted and bubbly.
7. **Slice and serve:**
   - Remove the garlic bread from the oven and let it cool for a minute or two. Slice into individual portions and serve warm.

Tips:

- **Variations:** You can customize your garlic bread by adding shredded mozzarella or other cheeses on top before baking for a cheesy garlic bread. You can also sprinkle with additional chopped herbs like basil or oregano for extra flavor.
- **Herb butter:** If you prefer, you can use a combination of herbs such as basil, thyme, or rosemary in your garlic butter mixture for a different flavor profile.
- **Make-ahead:** Prepare the garlic butter mixture in advance and store it in the refrigerator until ready to use. Spread on the bread and bake just before serving.

Garlic bread is a simple yet delicious addition to any meal, from pasta dishes to soups or salads. It's sure to be a hit with family and friends alike. Enjoy this homemade garlic bread warm and fresh from the oven!

Chicken pot pie

Ingredients:

For the filling:

- 2 tablespoons unsalted butter
- 1 onion, diced
- 2 carrots, diced
- 2 celery stalks, diced
- 2 cloves garlic, minced
- 1/4 cup all-purpose flour
- 2 cups chicken broth
- 1 cup milk (whole or 2%)
- 2 cups cooked chicken, diced or shredded
- 1 cup frozen peas
- Salt and pepper, to taste
- 1 teaspoon dried thyme (or 1 tablespoon fresh thyme)
- 1/2 teaspoon dried rosemary
- 1/2 teaspoon dried sage

For the crust:

- 1 package (2 sheets) store-bought puff pastry or pie crust (thawed if frozen)
- 1 egg, beaten (for egg wash)

Instructions:

1. **Preheat the oven:** Preheat your oven to 375°F (190°C).
2. **Prepare the filling:**
    - In a large skillet or pot, melt the butter over medium heat. Add diced onion, carrots, and celery. Cook until vegetables are softened, about 5-7 minutes.
    - Add minced garlic and cook for another 1-2 minutes until fragrant.
    - Sprinkle flour over the vegetables and stir to coat. Cook for 1-2 minutes to cook out the raw flour taste.
3. **Make the sauce:**
    - Gradually whisk in the chicken broth and milk, stirring constantly to avoid lumps. Cook until the mixture thickens and comes to a simmer, about 5-7 minutes.
4. **Add chicken and vegetables:**
    - Stir in the cooked chicken, frozen peas, dried thyme, rosemary, sage, salt, and pepper. Taste and adjust seasoning if needed.
5. **Assemble the pie:**
    - Transfer the chicken filling to a 9-inch deep-dish pie dish or a similarly sized baking dish.
6. **Prepare the crust:**
    - Roll out the puff pastry or pie crust on a lightly floured surface if needed to fit over the pie dish. Place the rolled-out dough over the filling, trimming any excess dough and crimping the edges to seal.
7. **Bake the pot pie:**
    - Brush the top of the pastry with beaten egg for a golden finish.
    - Cut slits in the center of the pastry to allow steam to escape.

- Place the pot pie on a baking sheet (to catch any drips) and bake in the preheated oven for 30-35 minutes, or until the crust is golden brown and the filling is bubbly.
8. **Serve:**
    - Remove from the oven and let the chicken pot pie cool for a few minutes before serving.

Tips:

- **Make-ahead:** You can prepare the filling and assemble the pot pie up to a day in advance. Keep the filling and crust separate until ready to bake. Cover and refrigerate until ready to bake.
- **Variations:** Feel free to add other vegetables like potatoes, corn, or green beans to the filling. You can also use leftover cooked turkey instead of chicken for a turkey pot pie.
- **Leftovers:** Store any leftover chicken pot pie covered in the refrigerator for up to 3 days. Reheat in the oven at 350°F (175°C) until warmed through.

Chicken pot pie is a comforting and satisfying meal that's perfect for chilly days or anytime you're craving a hearty dish. Enjoy making this classic homemade chicken pot pie for your family and friends!

Cornbread

Ingredients:

- 1 cup yellow cornmeal
- 1 cup all-purpose flour

- 1/4 cup granulated sugar (adjust to taste, optional)
- 1 tablespoon baking powder
- 1/2 teaspoon baking soda
- 1/2 teaspoon salt
- 1 cup buttermilk (or substitute with 1 cup milk + 1 tablespoon vinegar or lemon juice)
- 1/2 cup unsalted butter, melted and cooled slightly
- 2 large eggs

Instructions:

1. **Preheat the oven:** Preheat your oven to 400°F (200°C). Grease a 9-inch square baking pan or a cast-iron skillet with butter or cooking spray.
2. **Mix dry ingredients:** In a large bowl, whisk together the cornmeal, flour, sugar (if using), baking powder, baking soda, and salt until well combined.
3. **Mix wet ingredients:** In another bowl, whisk together the buttermilk, melted butter, and eggs until smooth.
4. **Combine wet and dry ingredients:** Pour the wet ingredients into the bowl with the dry ingredients. Stir until just combined. Do not overmix; a few lumps are okay.
5. **Bake:** Pour the batter into the prepared baking pan or skillet, spreading it evenly.
6. **Bake:** Bake in the preheated oven for 20-25 minutes, or until the cornbread is golden brown on top and a toothpick inserted into the center comes out clean.
7. **Cool and serve:** Remove from the oven and let the cornbread cool in the pan for 10 minutes before slicing and serving.

Tips:

- **Variations:** You can customize your cornbread by adding ingredients like chopped jalapeños, shredded cheese, or cooked bacon for extra flavor.
- **Serving suggestions:** Serve cornbread warm with butter, honey, or alongside chili, soups, or stews. It's also great for making cornbread stuffing or croutons for salads.
- **Storage:** Store leftover cornbread in an airtight container at room temperature for up to 3 days. It can also be frozen for longer storage.

Cornbread is a classic comfort food that's easy to make and always a crowd-pleaser. Enjoy this homemade cornbread recipe for a taste of Southern hospitality!

Mini quiches

Ingredients:

- 1 package (14 oz) pre-made pie dough (or use homemade pie crust)
- 4 large eggs

- 1/2 cup milk (whole milk or half-and-half)
- Salt and pepper, to taste
- 1/2 cup shredded cheese (such as cheddar, Swiss, or Gruyère)
- Fillings of your choice: chopped cooked bacon, diced ham, cooked spinach, diced bell peppers, caramelized onions, chopped herbs, etc.

Instructions:

1. **Preheat the oven:** Preheat your oven to 375°F (190°C). Lightly grease a mini muffin tin.
2. **Prepare the pie dough:** Roll out the pie dough on a lightly floured surface. Using a round cookie cutter or the rim of a glass, cut out circles of dough slightly larger than the diameter of each muffin cup.
3. **Line the muffin tin:** Press each circle of dough into the greased mini muffin cups, forming little tart shells. Prick the bottom of each shell with a fork to prevent air bubbles.
4. **Prepare the filling:** In a bowl, whisk together the eggs, milk, salt, and pepper until well combined. Stir in the shredded cheese and your choice of fillings (bacon, ham, spinach, etc.).
5. **Fill the tart shells:** Spoon the egg mixture evenly into each tart shell, filling almost to the top.
6. **Bake:** Bake in the preheated oven for 15-20 minutes, or until the quiches are set and the crust is golden brown.
7. **Cool and serve:** Remove from the oven and let the mini quiches cool in the muffin tin for a few minutes. Use a knife or spoon to carefully remove them from the muffin tin. Serve warm or at room temperature.

Tips:

- **Variations:** Experiment with different fillings to suit your taste. Vegetarian options can include sautéed mushrooms, diced tomatoes, or roasted vegetables.
- **Make-ahead:** Mini quiches can be made ahead of time and stored in an airtight container in the refrigerator. Reheat in the oven at 350°F (175°C) for a few minutes before serving.
- **Freezing:** Mini quiches can also be frozen after baking. Place them in a single layer on a baking sheet and freeze until firm. Transfer to a freezer bag or container for longer storage. Reheat from frozen in the oven at 350°F (175°C) until warmed through.

Mini quiches are versatile, portable, and always a hit at gatherings. Enjoy these delicious mini quiches as a savory snack or appetizer for any occasion!

Beef stew

Ingredients:

- 2 lbs stewing beef, cut into 1-inch cubes
- 2 tablespoons all-purpose flour

- Salt and pepper, to taste
- 2 tablespoons vegetable oil or olive oil
- 1 onion, chopped
- 2-3 cloves garlic, minced
- 4 cups beef broth (or stock)
- 1 cup red wine (optional, can substitute with more beef broth)
- 2 bay leaves
- 1 teaspoon dried thyme
- 1 teaspoon dried rosemary
- 4-5 medium carrots, peeled and cut into 1-inch pieces
- 4-5 medium potatoes, peeled and cut into 1-inch pieces
- 1 cup frozen peas (optional)
- Chopped fresh parsley, for garnish (optional)

Instructions:

1. **Prepare the beef:**
    - In a large bowl, toss the beef cubes with flour, salt, and pepper until evenly coated.
2. **Brown the beef:**
    - In a large Dutch oven or heavy-bottomed pot, heat the oil over medium-high heat. Add the beef cubes in batches, making sure not to overcrowd the pot. Brown the beef on all sides, about 4-5 minutes per batch. Remove the browned beef cubes and set aside.
3. **Cook the aromatics:**
    - In the same pot, add the chopped onion and cook for 5-7 minutes until softened and translucent. Add the minced garlic and cook for another 1-2 minutes until fragrant.
4. **Deglaze the pot:**
    - Pour in the beef broth and red wine (if using), scraping up any browned bits from the bottom of the pot with a wooden spoon or spatula.
5. **Simmer the stew:**
    - Return the browned beef cubes to the pot. Add bay leaves, dried thyme, and dried rosemary. Bring the mixture to a boil, then reduce the heat to low. Cover and simmer for 1.5 to 2 hours, stirring occasionally, until the beef is tender.
6. **Add vegetables:**
    - Add the carrots and potatoes to the stew. Cover and simmer for another 30-40 minutes, or until the vegetables are fork-tender.
7. **Finish the stew:**
    - Stir in the frozen peas (if using) and cook for another 5 minutes until heated through. Taste and adjust seasoning with salt and pepper if needed.
8. **Serve:**
    - Remove the bay leaves. Ladle the beef stew into bowls and garnish with chopped fresh parsley if desired. Serve hot, accompanied by crusty bread or over cooked rice or mashed potatoes.

Tips:

- **Slow cooker option:** You can also make beef stew in a slow cooker. After browning the beef and cooking the aromatics, transfer everything to a slow cooker and cook on low for 6-8 hours or on high for 3-4 hours, adding the vegetables in the last 1-2 hours of cooking.
- **Storage:** Beef stew tastes even better the next day as the flavors meld together. Store leftovers in an airtight container in the refrigerator for up to 3-4 days or freeze for longer storage.

Beef stew is a classic comfort food that's satisfying and perfect for feeding a crowd or enjoying as a cozy meal at home. Enjoy making and savoring this homemade beef stew recipe!

Pumpkin soup

Ingredients:

- 2 tablespoons unsalted butter
- 1 onion, chopped
- 2 cloves garlic, minced

- 1 teaspoon ground cumin
- 1/2 teaspoon ground coriander
- 1/2 teaspoon ground nutmeg
- 1/4 teaspoon ground cinnamon
- 1/4 teaspoon cayenne pepper (optional, for a bit of heat)
- 4 cups pumpkin puree (canned or homemade)
- 4 cups vegetable or chicken broth
- 1 cup heavy cream or coconut milk (for a dairy-free option)
- Salt and pepper, to taste
- Optional garnishes: toasted pumpkin seeds, chopped fresh herbs (such as parsley or chives), a drizzle of cream or coconut milk

Instructions:

1. **Cook the aromatics:**
   - In a large pot or Dutch oven, melt the butter over medium heat. Add the chopped onion and cook until softened, about 5-7 minutes. Add the minced garlic and cook for another 1-2 minutes until fragrant.
2. **Add spices:**
   - Stir in the ground cumin, ground coriander, ground nutmeg, ground cinnamon, and cayenne pepper (if using). Cook for 1 minute until the spices are fragrant.
3. **Combine pumpkin and broth:**
   - Add the pumpkin puree and vegetable or chicken broth to the pot. Stir well to combine.
4. **Simmer the soup:**
   - Bring the mixture to a boil, then reduce the heat to low. Cover and simmer for 15-20 minutes, stirring occasionally.
5. **Blend the soup:**
   - Remove the pot from heat. Using an immersion blender, blend the soup until smooth and creamy. Alternatively, carefully transfer the soup in batches to a blender and blend until smooth. Be cautious with hot liquids in the blender.
6. **Add cream and season:**
   - Stir in the heavy cream or coconut milk to the blended soup. Season with salt and pepper to taste. Adjust the consistency with additional broth if desired.
7. **Serve:**
   - Ladle the pumpkin soup into bowls. Garnish with toasted pumpkin seeds, chopped fresh herbs, and a drizzle of cream or coconut milk if desired.

Tips:

- **Pumpkin puree:** You can use canned pumpkin puree or make your own by roasting and pureeing fresh pumpkin.
- **Variations:** Customize your pumpkin soup by adding roasted garlic, ginger, or a splash of maple syrup for sweetness.

- **Storage:** Store leftover pumpkin soup in an airtight container in the refrigerator for up to 4 days. Reheat gently on the stove before serving.

Pumpkin soup is a comforting and nutritious dish that's perfect for cooler weather. Enjoy this homemade pumpkin soup recipe as a starter or main course for a cozy meal at home!

Scones

Ingredients:

- 2 cups all-purpose flour
- 1/4 cup granulated sugar

- 1 tablespoon baking powder
- 1/2 teaspoon salt
- 1/2 cup cold unsalted butter, cut into small cubes
- 1/2 cup milk (plus extra for brushing)
- 1 large egg
- 1 teaspoon vanilla extract
- Optional add-ins: dried fruit (such as raisins or cranberries), chocolate chips, nuts, or citrus zest

Instructions:

1. **Preheat oven and prepare baking sheet:** Preheat your oven to 400°F (200°C). Line a baking sheet with parchment paper.
2. **Mix dry ingredients:** In a large bowl, whisk together the flour, sugar, baking powder, and salt until well combined.
3. **Cut in butter:** Add the cold butter cubes to the flour mixture. Use a pastry cutter or your fingers to quickly rub the butter into the flour until the mixture resembles coarse crumbs with some pea-sized pieces of butter remaining.
4. **Combine wet ingredients:** In a separate bowl, whisk together the milk, egg, and vanilla extract.
5. **Form dough:** Make a well in the center of the dry ingredients and pour in the wet ingredients. Gently stir with a wooden spoon or spatula until just combined. The dough should come together but still be slightly crumbly.
6. **Add optional add-ins:** If using any optional add-ins (such as dried fruit, chocolate chips, etc.), gently fold them into the dough.
7. **Shape and cut scones:** Transfer the dough onto a lightly floured surface. Pat the dough into a circle or rectangle about 1-inch thick. Use a sharp knife or a biscuit cutter to cut the dough into triangles or rounds.
8. **Bake:** Place the shaped scones onto the prepared baking sheet. Brush the tops lightly with milk for a golden finish. Bake in the preheated oven for 15-18 minutes, or until the scones are golden brown and cooked through.
9. **Cool and serve:** Remove from the oven and transfer the scones to a wire rack to cool slightly. Serve warm or at room temperature with butter, jam, or clotted cream.

Tips:

- **Handling the dough:** Be careful not to overwork the dough, as this can make the scones tough. Mix and knead the dough just until it comes together.
- **Variations:** Experiment with different flavors by adding lemon zest, orange zest, or spices like cinnamon or nutmeg to the dough. You can also substitute part of the flour with whole wheat flour for a heartier texture.
- **Storage:** Scones are best enjoyed fresh on the day they are made. However, you can store leftovers in an airtight container at room temperature for up to 2 days. Reheat briefly in the oven or microwave before serving.

Homemade scones are a classic baked treat that is simple to make and delicious to enjoy. Whether plain or customized with your favorite add-ins, these scones are sure to be a hit!

Pita pockets with hummus

Ingredients:

- 4 pita bread rounds (whole wheat or regular)
- 1 cup hummus (store-bought or homemade)

- Optional fillings: sliced cucumbers, cherry tomatoes, lettuce or spinach leaves, red onion slices, roasted red peppers, olives, feta cheese, grilled chicken or falafel

Instructions:

1. **Prepare the pita bread:**
   - Warm the pita bread rounds briefly in a toaster, oven, or microwave to make them soft and pliable. This step is optional but can make it easier to stuff the pockets.
2. **Slice open the pockets:**
   - Carefully slice open each pita bread round along one edge to create a pocket. Be careful not to tear the bread completely in half.
3. **Spread hummus:**
   - Spoon about 1/4 cup of hummus into each pita pocket, spreading it evenly along the inside of the bread.
4. **Add fillings:**
   - Fill each pita pocket with your choice of fillings. Layer in sliced cucumbers, cherry tomatoes, lettuce or spinach leaves, red onion slices, roasted red peppers, olives, crumbled feta cheese, and any protein like grilled chicken or falafel.
5. **Serve:**
   - Serve the stuffed pita pockets immediately, or wrap them in foil or parchment paper for a convenient on-the-go meal.

Tips:

- **Variations:** You can customize your pita pockets with different types of hummus (such as roasted red pepper or garlic hummus), or add additional toppings like avocado slices, shredded carrots, or sprouts.
- **Make-ahead:** Prepare the pita pockets ahead of time, but wait to add any moist ingredients like tomatoes or lettuce until just before serving to prevent them from making the bread soggy.
- **Storage:** If you need to store prepared pita pockets, wrap them tightly in plastic wrap or foil and refrigerate. They are best enjoyed fresh but will keep for up to a day.

Pita pockets with hummus are not only delicious but also versatile and easy to customize with your favorite ingredients. Enjoy these flavorful and nutritious pockets for a quick and satisfying meal!

Chocolate-dipped fruit

Ingredients:

- Fresh fruit of your choice (strawberries, bananas, pineapple, kiwi, grapes, etc.)
- High-quality chocolate (dark, milk, or white chocolate)

- Optional toppings: chopped nuts, shredded coconut, sprinkles, sea salt, etc.

Instructions:

1. **Prepare the fruit:**
   - Wash and thoroughly dry the fruit. Make sure the fruit is completely dry before dipping it in chocolate to prevent the chocolate from seizing.
2. **Melt the chocolate:**
   - Chop the chocolate into small pieces for easier melting. You can melt the chocolate using a double boiler or in the microwave:
     - **Double boiler method:** Place a heatproof bowl over a pot of simmering water (make sure the water doesn't touch the bottom of the bowl). Add the chopped chocolate to the bowl and stir occasionally until melted and smooth.
     - **Microwave method:** Place the chopped chocolate in a microwave-safe bowl and microwave in 30-second intervals, stirring between each interval, until melted and smooth.
3. **Dip the fruit:**
   - Hold each piece of fruit by its stem or using a toothpick or skewer (for smaller fruits like grapes or strawberries). Dip the fruit into the melted chocolate, swirling to coat evenly.
4. **Optional: Add toppings:**
   - Immediately after dipping, sprinkle the chocolate-covered fruit with your choice of toppings, such as chopped nuts, shredded coconut, sprinkles, or a pinch of sea salt.
5. **Set the chocolate:**
   - Place the chocolate-dipped fruit on a parchment-lined baking sheet or plate. Allow the chocolate to set at room temperature for about 15-30 minutes, or refrigerate for quicker setting.
6. **Serve and enjoy:**
   - Once the chocolate has set, arrange the chocolate-dipped fruit on a serving platter or enjoy them straight from the parchment paper. They are best served the same day.

Tips:

- **Variations:** Experiment with different types of chocolate (dark, milk, white) or combinations of fruits. You can also drizzle melted chocolate of a different color over the set chocolate for a decorative effect.
- **Storage:** Chocolate-dipped fruit is best enjoyed fresh but can be stored in an airtight container in the refrigerator for up to 1-2 days. Keep in mind that fruits with higher water content (like strawberries) may release moisture and affect the texture of the chocolate over time.

- **Presentation:** For a special touch, arrange the chocolate-dipped fruit on a platter and dust lightly with powdered sugar before serving. This adds an elegant finish to your homemade treat.

Chocolate-dipped fruit is not only delicious but also makes for a beautiful and impressive dessert or snack. Enjoy creating and sharing these delightful treats with friends and family!

Apple crisps

Ingredients:

For the filling:

- 4-5 medium apples (such as Granny Smith, Honeycrisp, or any firm variety), peeled, cored, and sliced
- 1 tablespoon lemon juice
- 1/4 cup granulated sugar
- 1/2 teaspoon ground cinnamon
- 1/4 teaspoon ground nutmeg
- 1 tablespoon all-purpose flour

For the crisp topping:

- 1/2 cup old-fashioned rolled oats
- 1/2 cup all-purpose flour
- 1/2 cup packed brown sugar
- 1/4 teaspoon salt
- 1/2 cup unsalted butter, cold and cut into small pieces

Optional:

- Vanilla ice cream or whipped cream, for serving

Instructions:

1. **Preheat the oven:** Preheat your oven to 350°F (175°C). Grease a baking dish or individual ramekins with butter or cooking spray.
2. **Prepare the apples:** In a large bowl, toss the sliced apples with lemon juice to prevent browning.
3. **Mix the filling:** In a small bowl, combine the granulated sugar, cinnamon, nutmeg, and flour. Sprinkle this mixture over the apples and toss until the apples are evenly coated.
4. **Make the crisp topping:** In another bowl, combine the rolled oats, flour, brown sugar, and salt. Cut in the cold butter using a pastry cutter, two forks, or your fingers until the mixture resembles coarse crumbs with pea-sized pieces of butter.
5. **Assemble the crisps:** Divide the apple mixture evenly among the prepared baking dish or ramekins. Sprinkle the crisp topping over the apples, covering them evenly.
6. **Bake:** Place the baking dish or ramekins on a baking sheet (to catch any drips) and bake in the preheated oven for 35-40 minutes, or until the topping is golden brown and the apples are tender and bubbly.
7. **Serve:** Remove from the oven and let the apple crisps cool slightly before serving. Serve warm, topped with a scoop of vanilla ice cream or a dollop of whipped cream if desired.

Tips:

- **Variations:** You can customize your apple crisps by adding chopped nuts (such as pecans or almonds) to the topping, or by mixing in other fruits like berries or pears with the apples.

- **Storage:** Apple crisps are best enjoyed fresh and warm from the oven. Leftovers can be stored in the refrigerator, covered, for up to 2-3 days. Reheat in the oven at 350°F (175°C) until warmed through before serving.
- **Gluten-free option:** Substitute gluten-free flour and certified gluten-free oats to make this recipe gluten-free.

Apple crisps are a comforting dessert that highlights the natural sweetness of apples with a crunchy topping. Enjoy making and savoring this homemade apple crisp recipe for a cozy treat!

Baked apples

Ingredients:

- 4 large apples (such as Granny Smith, Honeycrisp, or Fuji)
- 1/4 cup brown sugar, packed
- 1 teaspoon ground cinnamon
- 1/4 teaspoon ground nutmeg
- 2 tablespoons unsalted butter, cut into small pieces
- 1/2 cup water or apple cider
- Optional: Vanilla ice cream or whipped cream, for serving

Instructions:

1. **Preheat the oven:** Preheat your oven to 375°F (190°C). Grease a baking dish large enough to hold the apples.
2. **Prepare the apples:** Wash and core the apples using an apple corer or a paring knife, leaving the bottoms intact. You can peel the apples or leave the skins on, depending on your preference.
3. **Mix the filling:** In a small bowl, mix together the brown sugar, ground cinnamon, and ground nutmeg.
4. **Stuff the apples:** Place the cored apples in the greased baking dish. Divide the brown sugar mixture evenly among the apples, spooning it into the center of each apple. Top each apple with pieces of butter.
5. **Add liquid:** Pour the water or apple cider into the bottom of the baking dish around the apples. This will help keep the apples moist while baking.
6. **Bake:** Cover the baking dish with foil and bake in the preheated oven for 30-40 minutes, or until the apples are tender when pierced with a fork. Remove the foil during the last 10 minutes of baking to allow the tops of the apples to caramelize slightly.
7. **Serve:** Remove the baked apples from the oven and let them cool slightly before serving. Serve warm, drizzled with the syrup from the baking dish and topped with a scoop of vanilla ice cream or whipped cream if desired.

Tips:

- **Variations:** You can customize your baked apples by adding chopped nuts (such as walnuts or pecans) to the filling mixture or by adding dried fruit (like raisins or cranberries).
- **Spiced option:** For a spiced variation, add a pinch of ground cloves or ginger to the brown sugar mixture.
- **Storage:** Baked apples are best enjoyed fresh and warm from the oven. Leftovers can be stored in the refrigerator, covered, for up to 2-3 days. Reheat in the oven or microwave until warmed through before serving.

Baked apples are a comforting and versatile dessert that highlights the natural flavors of the fruit with warm spices and a buttery sweetness. Enjoy making and savoring this homemade baked apple recipe for a cozy treat!

Spinach and cheese triangles

Ingredients:

- 1 package (about 16 oz) frozen phyllo dough, thawed according to package instructions

- 10 oz fresh spinach, washed and finely chopped (or use frozen spinach, thawed and drained)
- 1 cup crumbled feta cheese
- 1/2 cup ricotta cheese (optional, for creaminess)
- 1/2 cup grated Parmesan cheese
- 1 small onion, finely chopped
- 2 cloves garlic, minced
- 1/4 cup fresh dill, chopped (or use 1 tablespoon dried dill)
- 1/4 cup fresh parsley, chopped
- 1/4 cup olive oil, plus more for brushing
- Salt and pepper, to taste
- 1/2 teaspoon ground nutmeg (optional)
- Melted butter, for brushing (optional)

Instructions:

1. **Prepare the filling:**
   - If using fresh spinach, wash and finely chop it. If using frozen spinach, thaw it and squeeze out excess water.
   - In a large skillet, heat 1 tablespoon of olive oil over medium heat. Add the chopped onion and cook until softened, about 5 minutes. Add the minced garlic and cook for another 1-2 minutes until fragrant.
   - Add the chopped spinach to the skillet and cook, stirring occasionally, until wilted and any excess moisture has evaporated. Season with salt, pepper, and nutmeg (if using). Remove from heat and let cool slightly.
   - In a large bowl, combine the cooked spinach mixture with crumbled feta cheese, ricotta cheese (if using), grated Parmesan cheese, chopped dill, chopped parsley, and 1/4 cup of olive oil. Mix well to combine. Adjust seasoning to taste.
2. **Assemble the triangles:**
   - Preheat your oven to 375°F (190°C). Line a baking sheet with parchment paper.
   - Carefully unroll the phyllo dough and cover it with a damp kitchen towel to keep it from drying out.
   - Take one sheet of phyllo dough and brush it lightly with melted butter or olive oil. Fold the sheet in half lengthwise.
   - Place a spoonful of the spinach and cheese filling at one end of the folded phyllo strip, leaving a small border. Fold one corner of the phyllo over the filling to form a triangle. Continue folding the strip, maintaining the triangle shape, until you reach the end of the strip. Brush the completed triangle with more melted butter or olive oil.
   - Repeat with the remaining phyllo dough sheets and filling mixture until all the filling is used up.
3. **Bake the triangles:**
   - Place the assembled spinach and cheese triangles on the prepared baking sheet. Bake in the preheated oven for 20-25 minutes, or until the triangles are golden brown and crispy.

4. **Serve:**
    - Remove from the oven and let the triangles cool slightly before serving. Serve warm as an appetizer or snack.

Tips:

- **Phyllo dough handling:** Phyllo dough can dry out quickly, so work quickly and keep it covered with a damp towel when not using. If the edges of the phyllo sheets become dry or brittle, you can trim them off with a sharp knife.
- **Make-ahead:** You can assemble the spinach and cheese triangles ahead of time and freeze them before baking. When ready to bake, brush with butter or olive oil and bake from frozen, adding a few extra minutes to the baking time.
- **Variations:** Feel free to customize the filling with additional herbs (such as mint or basil) or add a pinch of red pepper flakes for a bit of heat.

Spinach and cheese triangles are a flavorful and satisfying dish, perfect for entertaining or enjoying as a delicious snack. They pair wonderfully with a side of tzatziki sauce or a fresh salad. Enjoy making and sharing these homemade spinach and cheese triangles!

Lentil soup

Ingredients:

- 1 cup dried lentils (brown or green), rinsed and picked over
- 1 tablespoon olive oil

- 1 onion, chopped
- 2 carrots, peeled and diced
- 2 celery stalks, diced
- 3 cloves garlic, minced
- 1 teaspoon ground cumin
- 1 teaspoon ground coriander
- 1/2 teaspoon smoked paprika (optional, for extra flavor)
- 1 bay leaf
- 6 cups vegetable or chicken broth
- 1 (14 oz) can diced tomatoes, with juices
- Salt and pepper, to taste
- Fresh lemon juice, to taste (optional, for brightness)
- Fresh parsley or cilantro, chopped (for garnish)
- Optional toppings: Greek yogurt or sour cream, croutons, or a drizzle of olive oil

Instructions:

1. **Prepare the lentils:** Rinse the lentils under cold water and pick through to remove any debris or stones. Set aside.
2. **Saute aromatics:** In a large pot or Dutch oven, heat the olive oil over medium heat. Add the chopped onion, carrots, and celery. Cook, stirring occasionally, until the vegetables are softened, about 5-7 minutes. Add the minced garlic, ground cumin, ground coriander, and smoked paprika (if using). Cook for another 1-2 minutes until fragrant.
3. **Simmer soup:** Add the rinsed lentils, bay leaf, vegetable or chicken broth, and diced tomatoes (with their juices) to the pot. Stir to combine. Bring the mixture to a boil, then reduce the heat to low. Cover and simmer for 25-30 minutes, or until the lentils and vegetables are tender.
4. **Season:** Once the lentils are tender, season the soup with salt and pepper to taste. Add a squeeze of fresh lemon juice for brightness, if desired.
5. **Serve:** Remove the bay leaf from the soup. Ladle the lentil soup into bowls and garnish with chopped fresh parsley or cilantro. Serve hot, optionally topped with a dollop of Greek yogurt or sour cream, croutons, or a drizzle of olive oil.

Tips:

- **Texture:** For a thicker soup, use an immersion blender to partially blend the soup, or mash some of the lentils against the side of the pot with a spoon.
- **Variations:** Customize your lentil soup by adding diced potatoes, chopped spinach or kale, or a splash of coconut milk for creaminess.
- **Storage:** Lentil soup keeps well in the refrigerator for up to 4-5 days. It also freezes well; let it cool completely before transferring to airtight containers or freezer bags for up to 3 months.

Lentil soup is not only comforting and delicious but also packed with protein, fiber, and essential nutrients. Enjoy this homemade lentil soup recipe as a nutritious meal on its own or paired with crusty bread for a satisfying lunch or dinner!

Stuffed zucchini boats

Ingredients:

- 4 medium zucchini
- 1 tablespoon olive oil
- 1 small onion, finely chopped
- 2 cloves garlic, minced
- 1 red bell pepper, diced
- 1 cup cooked quinoa or rice
- 1 (15 oz) can black beans, drained and rinsed
- 1 teaspoon ground cumin
- 1 teaspoon chili powder
- Salt and pepper, to taste
- 1 cup shredded cheese (such as cheddar, mozzarella, or a blend)
- Optional toppings: chopped fresh cilantro, diced tomatoes, avocado slices, sour cream or Greek yogurt

Instructions:

1. **Prepare the zucchini boats:**
    - Preheat your oven to 400°F (200°C). Line a baking sheet with parchment paper.
    - Cut each zucchini in half lengthwise. Use a spoon to scoop out the flesh from the center of each zucchini half, leaving about 1/4-inch thick shell. Chop the scooped-out zucchini flesh and set aside.
2. **Prepare the filling:**
    - In a large skillet, heat the olive oil over medium heat. Add the chopped onion and cook until softened, about 5 minutes.
    - Add the minced garlic and diced red bell pepper to the skillet. Cook for another 2-3 minutes until the pepper begins to soften.
3. **Combine the filling:**
    - Stir in the cooked quinoa or rice, drained black beans, chopped zucchini flesh, ground cumin, and chili powder. Cook for 2-3 minutes, stirring occasionally, until heated through. Season with salt and pepper to taste.
4. **Assemble and bake:**
    - Place the hollowed-out zucchini halves on the prepared baking sheet. Divide the filling mixture evenly among the zucchini boats, pressing gently to pack it in.
    - Sprinkle shredded cheese over the top of each stuffed zucchini boat.
5. **Bake:** Transfer the baking sheet to the preheated oven and bake for 20-25 minutes, or until the zucchini is tender and the cheese is melted and bubbly.
6. **Serve:** Remove from the oven and let the stuffed zucchini boats cool slightly before serving. Garnish with chopped fresh cilantro, diced tomatoes, avocado slices, and a dollop of sour cream or Greek yogurt if desired.

Tips:

- **Variations:** Feel free to customize the filling with your favorite ingredients such as ground meat (like turkey or chicken), mushrooms, spinach, or different types of beans.

- **Make-ahead:** You can prepare the filling and hollow out the zucchini ahead of time. Store the filling and zucchini halves separately in the refrigerator, then assemble and bake when ready.
- **Storage:** Stuffed zucchini boats can be stored in an airtight container in the refrigerator for up to 3 days. Reheat in the oven or microwave until heated through before serving.

Stuffed zucchini boats are a healthy and satisfying dish that's perfect for a light lunch or dinner. Enjoy this homemade recipe packed with nutritious ingredients!

Energy balls

Ingredients:

- 1 cup rolled oats
- 1/2 cup nut butter (such as almond butter, peanut butter, or sunflower seed butter)
- 1/4 cup honey or maple syrup
- 1/4 cup ground flaxseed or chia seeds
- 1/2 cup add-ins (such as chopped nuts, seeds, dried fruits, chocolate chips, or coconut flakes)
- 1 teaspoon vanilla extract
- Pinch of salt

Instructions:

1. **Combine dry ingredients:** In a large bowl, combine rolled oats, ground flaxseed or chia seeds, add-ins (nuts, seeds, dried fruits, etc.), and a pinch of salt. Stir to mix well.
2. **Add wet ingredients:** Add nut butter, honey or maple syrup, and vanilla extract to the bowl. Stir until all ingredients are thoroughly combined. The mixture should be sticky and hold together when pressed.
3. **Chill the mixture:** Cover the bowl and place it in the refrigerator for 30 minutes to 1 hour. Chilling helps the mixture firm up, making it easier to shape into balls.
4. **Shape into balls:** Remove the chilled mixture from the refrigerator. Using clean hands, scoop out about 1 tablespoon of the mixture and roll it into a ball between your palms. Repeat with the remaining mixture to form energy balls.
5. **Optional coating:** If desired, you can roll the energy balls in additional toppings such as shredded coconut, cocoa powder, or finely chopped nuts for added flavor and texture.
6. **Store:** Place the energy balls in an airtight container and store in the refrigerator for up to 1-2 weeks. You can also freeze them for longer storage.

Tips:

- **Customize:** Feel free to customize your energy balls with different nut butters, sweeteners, and add-ins based on your preferences. Experiment with combinations like almond butter with dried cherries and dark chocolate chips, or peanut butter with raisins and sunflower seeds.
- **Texture:** If the mixture seems too dry, add a bit more nut butter or honey/maple syrup. If it's too wet, add more oats or flaxseed/chia seeds.
- **Portable snack:** Energy balls are perfect for a quick snack on the go, pre or post-workout fuel, or a healthy treat between meals.

This basic recipe for energy balls is versatile and can be adapted to suit various dietary preferences and flavor profiles. Enjoy making and snacking on these homemade energy-packed treats!

Potato pancakes

Ingredients:

- 4 medium russet potatoes (about 2 lbs), peeled
- 1 small onion
- 2 large eggs, lightly beaten
- 3 tablespoons all-purpose flour or matzo meal
- 1 teaspoon salt, or to taste
- 1/2 teaspoon black pepper, or to taste
- Vegetable oil, for frying

Instructions:

1. **Grate the potatoes and onion:** Using a box grater or a food processor fitted with a grating blade, grate the potatoes and onion. Place the grated potatoes and onion in a clean kitchen towel or cheesecloth and squeeze out excess moisture. Transfer to a large bowl.
2. **Combine ingredients:** To the grated potatoes and onion, add the lightly beaten eggs, flour or matzo meal, salt, and black pepper. Mix well until everything is evenly combined.
3. **Heat the oil:** In a large skillet, heat about 1/4 inch of vegetable oil over medium-high heat until hot but not smoking.
4. **Form and fry the pancakes:** Take a heaping tablespoonful of the potato mixture and carefully place it into the hot oil, flattening it slightly with the back of the spoon to form a pancake shape. Repeat, leaving some space between each pancake in the skillet.
5. **Fry until golden brown:** Fry the potato pancakes for about 3-4 minutes on each side, or until they are golden brown and crispy. Use a spatula to carefully flip them over halfway through cooking.
6. **Drain and serve:** Once cooked, transfer the potato pancakes to a plate lined with paper towels to drain excess oil. Continue frying the remaining potato mixture in batches, adding more oil to the skillet as needed.
7. **Serve:** Serve the potato pancakes hot, garnished with applesauce, sour cream, or your favorite toppings. They are best enjoyed immediately while still warm and crispy.

Tips:

- **Keep warm:** If making a large batch, you can keep the cooked potato pancakes warm in a low oven (around 200°F / 93°C) on a baking sheet lined with parchment paper until ready to serve.
- **Variations:** You can customize your potato pancakes by adding grated carrots, finely chopped herbs (such as parsley or dill), or a sprinkle of garlic powder for extra flavor.
- **Make ahead:** While best served fresh, you can prepare the potato mixture in advance and fry the pancakes just before serving to maintain their crispiness.

Potato pancakes are a comforting and versatile dish that can be enjoyed as a side dish, appetizer, or even a light meal. They are a favorite in many cuisines and are sure to be a hit at any gathering or family meal. Enjoy making and savoring these homemade potato pancakes!

Rainbow salad

Ingredients:

- 1 cup cherry tomatoes, halved

- 1 cup red bell pepper, thinly sliced
- 1 cup orange bell pepper, thinly sliced
- 1 cup yellow bell pepper, thinly sliced
- 1 cup cucumber, thinly sliced or diced
- 1 cup shredded purple cabbage
- 1 cup shredded carrots
- 1/2 cup red onion, thinly sliced (optional)
- 1 avocado, diced (optional)
- 1/4 cup fresh herbs (such as cilantro, parsley, or basil), chopped
- 1/4 cup nuts or seeds (such as sliced almonds, pumpkin seeds, or sunflower seeds)
- Juice of 1 lemon or lime
- 2 tablespoons olive oil
- Salt and pepper, to taste

Instructions:

1. **Prepare the vegetables:** Wash and prepare all the vegetables and fruits as needed. Cut them into bite-sized pieces or slices according to your preference.
2. **Assemble the salad:** Arrange the prepared vegetables and fruits in a large salad bowl or platter in rows or groups to create a rainbow effect. Start with cherry tomatoes (red), followed by red bell pepper, orange bell pepper, yellow bell pepper, cucumber, purple cabbage, and shredded carrots.
3. **Add optional ingredients:** Scatter thinly sliced red onion and diced avocado (if using) over the salad. Sprinkle chopped fresh herbs and nuts or seeds on top for added flavor and texture.
4. **Make the dressing:** In a small bowl, whisk together the lemon or lime juice, olive oil, salt, and pepper until well combined. Drizzle the dressing over the salad just before serving.
5. **Serve:** Toss gently to coat the salad with the dressing. Serve immediately as a colorful and nutritious side dish or main meal.

Tips:

- **Variations:** Feel free to customize your rainbow salad by adding other colorful vegetables or fruits such as radishes, beets, mango, strawberries, or blueberries. You can also include cooked grains like quinoa or farro for added substance.
- **Make ahead:** You can prepare the ingredients ahead of time but assemble the salad and add the dressing just before serving to keep it fresh and crisp.
- **Presentation:** Arrange the salad on a large platter or individual plates to showcase the vibrant colors of the vegetables and fruits.

Rainbow salads are not only visually appealing but also packed with vitamins, minerals, and antioxidants from the variety of colorful ingredients. Enjoy creating and serving this nutritious and delicious rainbow salad!

Fruit crêpes

Ingredients:

For the crêpe batter:

- 1 cup all-purpose flour
- 2 large eggs
- 1 cup milk (whole or 2%)
- 1/4 cup water
- 2 tablespoons melted butter, plus extra for cooking
- 1 tablespoon granulated sugar (optional)
- 1/2 teaspoon vanilla extract (optional)
- Pinch of salt

For the filling:

- Fresh fruit of your choice (such as strawberries, blueberries, raspberries, bananas, or any seasonal fruit)
- Whipped cream, yogurt, or Nutella (optional, for spreading on the crêpes)

Instructions:

1. **Make the crêpe batter:**
   - In a large mixing bowl, whisk together the flour, eggs, milk, water, melted butter, sugar (if using), vanilla extract (if using), and salt until smooth. Let the batter rest for at least 30 minutes at room temperature (or refrigerate for up to 2 days).
2. **Cook the crêpes:**
   - Heat a non-stick skillet or crêpe pan over medium heat. Brush the pan lightly with melted butter.
   - Pour about 1/4 cup of batter into the center of the skillet, swirling the pan quickly to spread the batter evenly into a thin circle.
   - Cook the crêpe for about 1-2 minutes, or until the edges start to lift away from the pan and the bottom is lightly golden. Flip the crêpe using a spatula and cook for another 1-2 minutes on the other side.
   - Transfer the cooked crêpe to a plate and cover with a clean kitchen towel to keep warm. Repeat with the remaining batter, brushing the pan with more butter as needed. Stack the crêpes on top of each other as you cook.
3. **Prepare the filling:**
   - Wash and prepare the fresh fruit as needed. Slice larger fruits into bite-sized pieces.
   - If desired, spread a thin layer of whipped cream, yogurt, or Nutella on each crêpe before adding the fruit.
4. **Assemble the crêpes:**
   - Place a crêpe flat on a serving plate. Arrange a portion of the fresh fruit in the center of the crêpe.
   - Fold or roll the crêpe around the fruit, creating a neat package.
   - Repeat with the remaining crêpes and fruit.
5. **Serve:**
   - Serve the fruit crêpes immediately, optionally dusted with powdered sugar or drizzled with chocolate sauce or honey.

Tips:

- **Variations:** Experiment with different fruit combinations and fillings. You can also add a sprinkle of cinnamon or a splash of citrus juice to the fruit for extra flavor.
- **Make ahead:** You can prepare the crêpe batter in advance and refrigerate it for up to 2 days. Cook the crêpes just before serving for the best texture.
- **Presentation:** Arrange the filled crêpes on a platter or individual plates. Garnish with additional fresh fruit or mint leaves for a decorative touch.

Fruit crêpes are a versatile and delicious dessert that's perfect for any occasion. Enjoy making these homemade crêpes filled with your favorite fresh fruits for a delightful treat!

www.ingramcontent.com/pod-product-compliance
Lightning Source LLC
LaVergne TN
LVHW061943070526
838199LV00060B/3954